A PARTY FAVOR

Based on a series of experimental parties given by the famous Gesell Institute, this remarkably specific how-to-do-it guide describes what works and what doesn't *in actual practice* at parties for youngsters from three to fifteen.

THE GESELL INSTITUTE PARTY BOOK highlights with practical examples the different things which make a party a success at each successive age.

The delightful and informative photographs made by the *Life* staff at actual parties conducted and supervised by the Gesell Institute add uniquely to the value of the book and show the joy of party-giving for young and old.

The Gesell Institute
PARTY BOOK

Frances L. Ilg, M.D.

Louise Bates Ames, Ph.D.
Authors of *Child Behavior*

and

Evelyn W. Goodenough, Ph.D.

Irene B. Andresen, M.A.

A DELL BOOK

PUBLISHED BY
DELL PUBLISHING CO., INC.
750 THIRD AVENUE
NEW YORK 17, N. Y.

COPYRIGHT © 1956, BY THE GESELL INSTITUTE
OF CHILD DEVELOPMENT, INC.
DELL ® TM 681510, DELL PUBLISHING CO., INC.
ALL RIGHTS RESERVED

REPRINTED BY ARRANGEMENT WITH
HARPER & BROTHERS
NEW YORK, N. Y.

FIRST DELL PRINTING—DECEMBER, 1963

PRINTED IN U.S.A.

Contents

Contents

Acknowledgments

Grateful acknowledgment is made to *Life* magazine not only for its inception of the idea and its substantial contribution in photographing party behavior at five of the ages in question, but for its permission to use a selection of these photographs. We especially wish to express appreciation to photographers Nina Leen, Walter Sanders, Alfred Eisenstaedt, Tana Hobin, and Yale Joel.

We are also extremely grateful to the many parents who co-operated in giving the parties which we have described, and to the children who took part and who in spite of observers and photographers helped us by behaving so unself-consciously, naturally, and characteristically.

But most of all we wish to express our appreciation to reporter Susan Neuberger, who gave the parties their continuity through her tireless effort and who seemed capable of surmounting any difficulties.

Preface

"A number of years ago I read with a great deal of interest your series of articles on children's parties in *Life* magazine. This week I gave a party for my 4-year-old twins according to your rules. This party was so successful that I would like to have the rules for the other parties if you could send them to me."

We should like to answer this mother's letter, and the many other requests which we have received since the publication of the *Life* series, in this book, illustrated with the original *Life* photographs.

We cannot absolutely guarantee that a reading of this book, and an application of the rules it gives, will bring you the glowing tributes from your party guests that we received when giving the original parties: "The best party I ever went to"; "The most wonderful experience of my life!"; "Boy! This really *is* a party!" But we do believe that if you follow our general rules, you at least will not end up with the guests in tears or tatters, and with yourself determined never to give another party.

A little knowledge of the age in question can in most instances do more than a large expenditure of time, money, and energy in making your children's parties a success—both for them and for their guests.

This present volume, though it indicates in some detail and

rather specifically the kinds of games and even the order of games which may be played at parties, is not intended primarily as a manual of games. Its primary emphasis is on the kinds of behavior which may be expected of children of different ages in a party situation. It aims to indicate the kinds of party situations in which different aged children can take part successfully and enjoyably. It particularly emphasizes danger points and things to be avoided as too complex and too difficult at certain ages.

In short, though the setting of behavior described here is the party situation, the theme of this book is, as in our other publications, child behavior.

Also, though we have selected certain games and activities as being especially effective and desirable at certain age levels, many of the games here described could be introduced effectively throughout a fairly wide age range. Musical Chairs, for instance, is enjoyed by children of many different ages. Bowling would be a good activity at other ages than eight. Or, a Valentine or Halloween party is appropriate not just to the ages where we have placed it, but to almost any age. But the game will be played differently, the entertainment value of the special-occasion party will be different, depending on the age of the child guests.

Perhaps more important than knowing just which activities will probably be successful at any specific age is a general attitude toward child behavior which we have tried to convey in this book—both in text and pictures. This attitude emphasizes an appreciation of the fact that child behavior has shape and integrity, and that it tends to change in a predictable, patterned way as a child grows older. Adults who have this attitude toward children attempt, within reason, to fit the demands of any given situation—in this instance a party—to a child's abilities and inabilities, rather than setting up the situation arbitrarily and then demanding that the child conform.

A party situation, much as most children love it, is not always easy for them. An appreciation of age factors can help reduce chaos, confusion, and disappointment by providing, at succeeding ages, those environmental factors which a child can meet, and avoiding those which will make too great demands.

However, at parties as at school or in everyday home situations, it is never enough for the adult in charge to follow blindly a blueprint or set of rules. More important than rules in helping children to have a good time is a real love of children, an understanding of them, a warmth, and an appreciation that children are not puppets to be manipulated, and that they do not all respond alike. Some have more social stamina than do others; some are more socially minded and more amenable than are others.

Not only do children behave differently in a party situation at different ages, but their demands of and response to the adult are different at different ages. Mothers are extremely important to many 3- and 4-year-olds, and some do better if Mother is right there at the party. Most 6-year-olds exhibit much better party behavior if Mother is not present. In the mid-teens, the presence of at least the host's parents is still necessary for practical purposes of providing refreshments and control, but otherwise the adult is largely ignored.

Thus one secret of success for a party-giver is to arrange what you believe the child needs, or at older ages the thing he says he needs, in the way of equipment, provision, and supervision, but not to try too hard to impose your ideas of what children should enjoy. A truly successful, suitable party at any age can provide such pleasure, not only for the guests but for the adults in charge, that it is well worth careful planning. And by taking just a little thought, rather than leaving it up to fate that everything will be well accepted and everyone will have a good time, you will have done a great deal to insure a successful party.

Though individual children do, of course, differ in their rate of development, we believe that in general in the first eleven years, the parties we have suggested will be suitable at the ages we have indicated. From eleven on, there will be some differences in different communities, and among different groups of children, as to the ages at which dancing parties can successfully start. We have heard of mothers of 10-year-olds who planned dancing parties for their children. This to us seems early. In other communities, dancing may not come in with much success until as late as fourteen. The teen-age and pre-teen-age parties which we have described were given successfully in New Haven, Connecticut, where most of the parties in this book took place.

But social maturity like all other aspects of behavior varies from child to child, as do also the fads and customs of various communities. It is important at older ages to find out from your son or daughter what kinds of parties boys and girls of his age and in your community like. Many older boys and girls will be socially mature enough to read this party book and to suggest which kind of party would be most suitable for them and their friends.

We close this preface with the note that some people don't seem to need a book to help them give successful parties. They appear to entertain as naturally and as effortlessly and as confidently as they breathe. However, especially for most of you, if the party in question is for a first or only child, that is, if you have not already had practical experience with the age in question, we believe that this book can be of real help.

The First Five Years

Birthdays are to celebrate. But how? For whom? The presence of the 1-year-old birthday child at his own party may be considered relatively unimportant. The occasion itself may be deemed sufficient for giving a party. But even the year-old child is capable of responding in his year-old way. Should he not be considered? Should not the occasion provide the basis for some memorable experience which can add to his storehouse of richly lived moments, even though he may not be able to recall it? Lights and movement are his great delight. These can be provided in one lighted candle. Perhaps he feels the atmosphere of the occasion. Perhaps he feels the love of his parents as this gift of warmth and light is presented. The moment is his, and his absorbed response, followed perhaps by vocal expressions of delight, attests to his enjoyment.

By two years of age much has happened; much social awareness and experience have been fostered. The 2-year-old may even know the meaning of the word "party." But this is no reason for the elaborate planning and execution of a 2-year-old party which all too often ends up with as many as twenty people of mixed ages, when there should have been closer to two. What inspires this lavish expansion is hard to tell; but it does happen over and over again. It was the devastating failure of just such a party that inspired the quest undertaken in this book.

A party for a 2-year-old is best planned with his social immaturity clearly in mind. His concept of "party" is perhaps most closely allied to "tea party," in which the sheer manipulation of dishes and the pouring of liquid make the party a party. He is beginning to know the word "present," and can enjoy tearing paper off his gifts, though with some help. What better gift could he have, boy or girl, than a tea set and an appreciative small audience which can respond to him at his own level? One grandmother added to the family group may be quite enough in the way of guests—someone who will not hurry him, someone who can respond to each dish removal, someone who will join him in his idea of pouring milk and eating cookies—one for each hand, please!

If we are successful with our children's first and second birthday parties, we can anticipate further successes. We will certainly discard from our minds that static concept of a party as simply the gathering together of a lot of children—a concept which unfortunately has produced more dismal failures than successes.

Thus we may ask—should any children be invited to a 3-year-old's birthday celebration? Might not a favorite adult—a baby sitter, a relative, a neighbor—bring the needed party spirit that will delight the party child and make the occasion his very own? And keep in mind that it is not only at three years of age, but at any age from preschool through adolescence, that the parent needs to help decide whether the more usual party is actually the best way for the child to celebrate his birthday. There are so many different ways of celebrating. A special outing with one or two good friends may provide by far the most satisfactory occasion at some ages. Such an outing may include a visit to a zoo or museum, a train ride, a movie, a trip to a hobby shop with money for both birthday child and guest to spend as they choose, lunch at a favorite restaurant, or perhaps a skiing, swimming, or other sports trip. These are only a few of many different possibilities provided by different communities. Parents need not be slaves to traditional yearly birthday parties.

The advisability of a party for a 3-year-old is dependent to a large extent on the kind of group experience the child has had. Is he an only child who has known only adult birthday celebrations, or is he one of several children already familiar with birthday cakes, songs, and the opening of presents? What has been his group experience in the neighborhood, in nursery school, in Sunday school? Since THREE has not yet begun to think of this next milestone, nor of parties as such, he needs a perceptive parent to decide what will provide the best birthday celebration for him.

But by four the child is well aware that on his birthday he will be a year older—will be four. This may inspire him to all sorts of heroic planning, such as that he will give up some of his more babyish ways. He may so fully experience his party in anticipation that he may be quite unable to cope with it when the time actually comes. Mothers need to be aware of this possible about-face. They need to realize that FOUR may very suddenly and dramatically object to anything that calls too much attention to himself, perhaps even the idea of a party that he has eagerly looked forward to for weeks.

This can mean that he may suddenly feel too much "in the limelight." Perhaps too much stress has been placed on his role as host and on how he should conduct himself at his party. He may even be reduced to tears if he is sung to or receives a birthday spanking. In such an event a mother needs to be ready to

3

jump right in and shift the course of activities in such a way as to de-emphasize the party child's role.

Most parents can predict how their children will respond, and will recognize that some FOURS are better off not going to parties, that others might suddenly become sick on the way to the party and thus need to be taken home, and that still others may produce such disruptive havoc that they should only attend a part of the party and then only under parental supervision. In these days of nursery schools, a happy solution for a 4-year-old party might be to have the party child bring cupcakes and napkins for the nursery-school group. The napkin becomes that tangible piece of party that can be slipped into a pocket and taken home. We know of one 4-year-old, whose birthday had been over-celebrated for four days with all kinds of parties and occasions, who suddenly burst into tears. His reason for crying was that he hadn't had a chance to bring cupcakes to school. This simple act would have been more satisfying to him than all of his parents' elaborate planning.

FIVE is much hardier, though often not so overtly enthusiastic. He takes a much more active part than does the younger child in the actual planning of the party, even in some detail. He may have definite ideas as to whom he wants to invite, what he wants to eat, what he wants to do. Parents need to be warned not to take him too literally, however, for his ideas often should be tempered a bit. If he goes to nursery school, a consultation with his teacher about his guest list might help to form a more cohesive group. The addition or omission of one child from the guest list can often mean the difference between a highly successful party and one that is wild and out-of-bounds.

THREE

The average 3-year-old is, at his best, a friendly, agreeable, sociable little creature. Not yet ready for complex or prolonged social interchange, he likes to play beside—if not at all times actively with—his contemporaries.

For the most part much less demanding, possessive, and grabby than he was six months earlier, he is still not beyond the age of fighting over possessions. The social activity of a group of THREES is likely to be marked by sudden squalls and squabbles, so that there still needs to be considerable supervision and occasional intervention by an adult close at hand.

THREE enjoys the notion of a party, but his actual ideas of "party" are vague and undemanding. A pleasant and brief opportunity to play at someone else's house, plenty of toys available, some simple refreshments and a gift or favor for himself will in most cases satisfy him better than any attempt to have him take part in games.

THREE loves surprises and things that are different. But he is not yet ready to appreciate or enjoy anything too complex in the way of a surprise.

Any group of 3-year-olds tends to vary tremendously in the social hardiness of its individual members. Mothers of more fragile—or wilder—children will need to accompany them on their social ventures at this age, standing ready to give support, or to calm things down, as the occasion may require. The length of time for which individual 3-year-olds can hold up socially also varies tremendously and should be kept in mind when the length of their stay at a party is being planned. An especially shy or difficult child might, for example, come late to a party.

Most mothers recognize the fact that many preschoolers are not at their best in a new social situation. For this reason, they do not consider it an adverse reflection on their upbringing of their child if quarrels and difficulties do arise. They simply and calmly separate children who are quarreling, support any child who is not holding up. Parties do not constitute an ideal situation for disciplining, so it is more important to settle quarrels quickly than always to settle them fairly. A difficult child should be removed from the scene of the difficulty rather than be punished or improved on the spot.

THREE-YEAR-OLD PARTY

Key

The secret of success for a 3-year-old party is to have the tempo very slow and the proceedings flexible and unregimented. THREE's expectations are not very high. He is not very demanding of a party. Mothers of extremely shy or boisterous children may need to stay for the entire party. Other mothers don't need to stay; in fact their children may behave better without them.

NUMBER OF GUESTS: Five or six children, both boys and girls.

NUMBER OF ADULTS: The host or hostess's mother and two or three other mothers.

Schedule

One and a half hours is a good length for this party. An ideal time is from 11:30 to 1 o'clock.

11:30–12:00   Arrival and informal play. A great deal of the party at this age consists of opening, looking at, and playing most informally with the presents and with the host's toys. Doors to the room where the party table is set, and to any other rooms which should not be entered, are shut. Otherwise guests are free to wander at will.

Each child usually likes to bring a present. Presents may be saved till all arrive, then all opened at once. However, the time or manner of opening presents doesn't really matter. Guests will be moderately interested in the present opening but are more interested in playing informally, especially in the playroom. Children play together some, but there is much solitary play. Mothers attend to children when necessary; otherwise talk to each other.

12:00–12:30   Refreshment time. The table is already set up in another room. Use paper plates, paper cups, paper napkins. Have a piece of candy (gumdrop or marshmallow) at each place. Just before the children go to the table, the mother hands around a basket with little favors for each (cars, dolls)—preferably all of the same kind. Balloon décor.

Children sit around a coffee table in small chairs (some borrowed if necessary). Refreshments consist of very small sandwiches and milk. Some children may wander away but will come back for the cake, which is served after the sandwiches are finished. The cake is shown and the candles blown out. Then the cake is cut on the sideboard, and each child is given a *small* piece. Children will eat the ice cream but may pay little attention to the cake. Mothers, standing around to supervise the eating, may themselves like to eat simple refreshments—sandwiches and coffee.

12:30–1:00   Informal play. A second basket of party gifts, one for each child, is brought in. These gifts may be little dolls in baskets for the girls, airplanes or cars for the boys. They each choose—a ribbon on each gift allows it to be pulled from the basket.

Children scatter around the living room and playroom. They sit on the floor with their gifts, rock on the rocking

7

horse, play with puzzles or other toys, or with crayons. Some may play the phonograph.

1:00   Mothers who did not stay return. All mothers gradually start getting outer clothing (if cold weather) on children. The décor balloons are taken down and there is one (all blown up and tied with a string) for each child as he or she leaves. This final present helps them to get out of the door happily.

Expenses

This can be an extremely inexpensive party. The chief expenses are the ice cream, cake, favors, and one or two small presents for each child. Five dollars might well cover the total expense.

Hints and Warnings

It is most important not to try to make this party too formal. Don't try to play games. Remember that a 3-year-old party at its best is an extremely relaxed, informal situation.

Be sure that there is a mother present for each shy or wild child. Have the mothers solve any problems which arise by separating the children involved—don't try to work out problems *fairly*. This is no time for good discipline, or for teaching moral lessons about sharing or about being a good host or hostess or a good guest. Remember that the host or hostess does not have to accept too much from the guests just because they are guests. Remember also that many quite good children behave their worst at a party.

Realize that by the end of the party all the children may be over-stimulated. Try to have the departures happy if possible. Final gifts help.

FOUR

Four is perhaps the first age when the very characteristics of the age lend themselves ideally to party-giving and party-going.

The average 2-year-old is not really certain what a party is. Is it the cake? The ice cream? The guests?

THREE enjoys a party more or less as he would a morning at nursery school or an afternoon of play with a friend. He is on

9

the verge of awareness that a party is something special and exciting, but often only on the verge.

Four, however, can be an ideal party age. The 4-year-old tends to be a creature of boundless energy, enthusiasm, and appetite for the new and different and exciting. He *loves* an occasion, and a party is just the kind of occasion which he loves best.

Parents often complain that FOUR tends to be out-of-bounds. True, but a party does not need to bring out this quality in him, since his out-of-bounds tendencies are most conspicuous when life is going badly or when he is being disciplined or ignored. FOUR's enthusiasm can be co-operative if things are exciting enough and are going his way. He tends to be extremely appreciative of adult attention. He throws himself fully and positively into plans for his own entertainment.

It is easy to entertain a 4-year-old if you yourself have the time, energy, good will, and imagination. He tends to accept quite uncritically the games you suggest, the food you serve, the favors and surprises which you provide. (FIVE may say, "Oh, I have one of those." THIRTEEN may mutter, "Oh, one of those!" Not so with the 4-year-old.) FOUR's demand for something special or something new and different is easily satisfied by simple favors or attractive decoration.

Discipline should not yet be a major problem, at least for the mother who understands children of this age. As at other ages, a party is not the place for lessons in sharing, behaving, minding. Quarrels should be settled as quickly and inconspicuously as possible by removing one of the quarrelers, or by providing some different but acceptable toy for one of the two grabbers.

Mother prepares

The party gets under way

Mother participates as needed

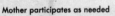

Comfort

Trouble

Cake and ice cream

Balloons to take home

FOUR-YEAR-OLD PARTY

Key

The keys to a successful party at this age are: speed, simplicity, novelty. Speed is necessary because the group itself is speedy. FOURS react quickly; and they tire rapidly if the party drags or if it lasts too long. Simplicity is important because children of this age are not mature enough to understand or to participate in complex games. Some novel element is important because FOURS, unlike THREES, have a notion of what a "party" is (even though perhaps only a vague one) and expect something other than just to go and play. This surprise should be something quite simple, such as a distribution of favors.

NUMBER OF GUESTS: Six guests is a good number, and not more than eight (both boys and girls). It may be safe to invite one or two extras, or at least to have some in mind who can be invited at the last minute. There are apt to be casualties among invited guests so that they do not get to the party. They may be ill from overexcitement, their mother may not be able to get a baby sitter and so cannot bring them, or other difficulties may get in the way.

NUMBER OF ADULTS: The host or hostess's mother and one adult helper need to be available. One or two of the mothers may need to stay, as at three—that is, mothers of children who are extremely shy or extremely aggressive, or who for other reasons may need their mothers to be there.

Schedule

One and a half hours is plenty, ideally from 3:30 to 5. This timing allows for a nap beforehand for those who still need one, yet doesn't bring the refreshments too near dinnertime.

3:30–4:10 Guests arrive and play with toys. Parents bring, or earlier may have brought over, something for each child to play with (in addition to what the home may provide) for this initial period. Thus the living room somewhat resembles a nursery-school playroom, with a good assortment of toys, including big cars and trains, a rocking horse, blackboard, dolls and carriages, stuffed animals, Blockraft, Tinkertoys, big musical tops. Children play, usually quite individually, with these toys. Host opens presents as they come.

4:10–4:15 As children go into room where refreshments are waiting, each one is given a favor. Fireman hats and badges make good favors. These may be available on a table, and are given to each child as he or she goes into the dining room.

4:15–4:40 Refreshments have been all set up in advance on card tables or on low children's tables. (Tables may have to be borrowed.) Use paper cloth, napkins, plates, bright cups. And provide some kind of favors—for instance, little toy frying pans filled with candy. Balloons—all blown up—hang in a cluster on the wall. These are given to the children toward the end of the party.

Refreshments consist of simple small sandwiches, the smaller the better, but in interesting shapes. Better for children to eat several small sandwiches apiece then to half-eat one big one. Or sandwiches can be omitted and you can have just ice cream, cake, and milk. Individual frosted cupcakes may be better for eating, but there should be a central cake with four candles on it, which can be blown out.

4:40–5:00 Informal play period. Children play with the toys in the living room and with balloons which have been distributed. (If balloon play becomes vigorous, it may be necessary to push toys to the edge of the room to allow space.)

At this time, also, there can be given out special surprise favors. These are wrapped separately and may be presented in a big cloth bag which the children reach into, taking turns. They unwrap and play with these. Good favors include: small figures of animals or humans, small balls with elastic, toy wrist watches, toy rings, fire trucks.

5:00 Departure. Mothers who are already there leave with their children. Other mothers call for their children. However, most Fours by the end of a party are tired and excitable and may cry or go to pieces if they have to wait to be called for. Thus it may have been arranged for the mothers already there to take all the children home.

Expenses

This can be an inexpensive party. Favors might cost around $2; refreshment, $3; balloons, 50¢. Total, around $5.

Hints and Warnings

Remember that you can count on only minimal group activity. Individual informal play is better than organized games. In fact, it is not only unnecessary but may be dangerous to introduce even simple games. Ring Around the Rosy or Farmer in the Dell would be better than something complex such as Pin the Tail on the Donkey—but we do not recommend having any games.

Every child is apt to think that it is *his* birthday, wish it were his birthday, or pretend that it is his. So all may want to blow out the candles and you may have to help the party child to blow. If someone else gets there first, you will have to relight the candles.

As at three, Mother can greet guests and thank them. She should not expect too much in the way of manners from either the host or the guests. Guests may want to take home the gifts they have brought. Or the birthday child may not allow anyone to touch his presents.

There are almost bound to be some tears, some spilling, some disagreements or quarreling. Be especially careful that the party does not last too long. Fours tire easily and become overexcited. Also a too-late party comes too near dinnertime.

Remember that more than eight guests is too many.

As to favors and gifts: if you have hats, sturdy homemade ones are better than purchased ones, which are apt to rip and tear. Blowers may become a menace as children blow them into each others' faces. Don't have favors, surprises, hats, etc., all at the refreshment table. It makes for too much confusion. Have the surprises spread out a bit through the party rather than giving them all at once.

FIVE

The 5-year-old often gives a somewhat deceptive appearance of being exceptionally self-contained and capable. Experience shows, however, that he seems capable because he normally does not try to do too much that is new or difficult. When faced with either the new or the difficult he may need a surprising amount of assistance. For this reason, the 5-year-old at a party, which presents new situations and opportunities to which he may not be accustomed, may need a good deal of adult help in taking part in games and in carrying out directions. This necessary help should be immediately available, or adults in charge may be surprised to see the usually collected FIVE go to pieces.

The 5-year-old is not an exceptionally sociable individual. Often if given a free choice he keeps pretty much to himself, especially in a strange situation. He may rely a good deal on a best friend, but just the notion of making friends for its own sake may have lost the charm it held a few months earlier. Thus it is important, at a party, not to count on too much interaction among guests, particularly until they get warmed up. They may need quite a prolonged warming-up period, so that it will usually work out best to provide initial activity which is more or less solitary and which does not require co-operation. Even once the party is well under way, it is safest not to expect too much collaborative activity.

Getting rid of excessive energy is already something of a problem at parties. (It will be even more so at later ages.) Thus it is wise to provide at least some games which involve considerable charging about the house.

FIVES have a strong property sense, but are not as yet capable of keeping track of their properties. Thus, as at the years which immediately follow, a good safe container, clearly marked, needs to be available for their prizes and products. The mother in charge must not only provide this container, but should also provide a good, safe, but conspicuous place to keep it. Then each child can keep his eye on his possessions at all times.

Well-behaved as the average 5-year-old is much of the time, a party does not always bring out his best behavior. As at earlier ages, any difficulties or disputes should be smoothed over as easily as possible, without emphasis on what adults may consider "proper" party behavior.

FIVE-YEAR-OLD PARTY

Key

The key to a successful 5-year-old party seems to be a great deal of planning in advance, even to the extent of overplanning. Have all materials and props ready beforehand. Have games and activities for every minute, and especially for the beginning and end of the party. There is likely to be little interaction among the children and little spontaneous activity. FIVES tend to behave in a rather solitary fashion, though there is a little talking and showing each other what they have been given or what they have made.

A big thing seems to be for each to be busy in more or less individual fashion, though all doing the same things. Also quite a bit of help or attention is needed from an adult.

Five-Year-Old Party

Some key *theme* helps to make the party exciting for them—a Valentine theme, St. Patrick's theme, Indian theme. . . .

NUMBER OF GUESTS: Six is probably a good number of guests, because FIVES find it hard to wait for turns or attention, as might be necessary when there are more. Preferably have guests of one sex only, though it will work out all right at this age if you have to have both boys and girls. The party described here is a girls' party.

NUMBER OF ADULTS: There should be at least two adults—the mother and one or two helpers.

Schedule

This party can last for two hours. A late-afternoon party ending with refreshments may be best.

4:00–4:15   Guests assemble. This period should be filled with some good planned activity, relatively quiet, relatively solitary. Some hand activity is good—making things with pipe cleaners or with clay, for instance. If possible this activity should be set up in advance in a place apart from the main party room or, if necessary, in a corner of the party room.

4:15–4:30   Game of Spider. This gives the children a chance to get acquainted with, or adjusted to, each other without demanding much mingling. Strings are wound around all through the house, in and out of the furniture. Each child follows her own string, winding it onto a little pasteboard spool which has been provided. Children climb in and out, over and under, but must not move the furniture. Finally, each finds a present at the end of her string. (Presents for this and other games can include any little things, as comb and brush for doll, doll jewelry, play make-up, coin purses, miniature animals, little banks, crayons.)

4:30–5:10   Game of Clues. Clues are written on red paper hearts (if a Valentine party; otherwise on some other item suitable to the kind of party being given). Mother reads aloud the clues which might be "under something yellow in the living room," "under something green in the front bedroom," etc. Whole group goes charging all over the house to find these successive clues. The last clue leads to a treasure for each person.

This treasure can be materials for making something: i.e., Valentine hats and aprons, or calendars, or pot holders, or candlestick holders. Preferably this should be something in keeping with the theme of the party.

All this charging around after the clues, especially if the party is held in a fairly large house, tires children out, and they are contented to sit fairly quietly making whatever their material suggests.

5:10–5:15   Marching and record playing. Fives love marching. A birthday march all around the area used for the party can be great fun. A phonograph record, a piano, or the singing of a rousing song can provide the musical background for the march. Simple rhythm instruments for each of the children add to the fun. This is an activity both boys and girls like and it gives a further opportunity to work off energy. Or some suitable record, preferably an "activity" record, can be played, so that the whole group can join in.

5:15–5:45   Refreshments. Table set ahead of time in the dining room—regular dining table. Tablecloth, napkins, plates of paper. Simple favors—perhaps special placecard holder for each child. Children's food tastes at this age tend to be conservative, so don't try anything fancy or give a choice of foods. A good menu includes small sandwiches, milk, and some crunchy food like carrot sticks or celery. End with cake and ice cream.

5:45–6:00   Some planned activity for after food—something to do till all parents arrive. Coloring or some other sedentary activity is good.

Expenses

The big expense here is the presents. These should not be too expensive individually, but they do come to quite a lot with all the material involved in making things. $10 to $15 should cover presents plus refreshments.

Hints and Warnings

It is very important to have all the many materials ready in advance, so that there will be no long waits. Fives need to be entertained steadily; they are not good at improvising, at least not while at a party.

21

Five-Year-Old Party

It is also important to plan some good thing which will get them started and will keep them occupied till all arrive, without much demand on them for spontaneity or sociability.

Six guests are probably enough, as it is very hard for children at this age to wait their turns. Also with such games as Spider, if there are too many guests, the party is just too complicated to prepare.

Be careful not to let expenses get out of hand. Remember that for each favor or gift you must multiply by the number of guests. Also that children this age like to make things but that they need a good deal of help.

Be *sure* to provide a good marked bag or container for their presents and favors. They become very much upset if they think their "things" are getting lost or mixed up with other people's.

Remember that the 5-year-old party is very important to FIVES, perhaps even more than the 4-year-old party is to FOURS. The child may have anticipated it so long that he or she may be overexcited, and thus you may have to overlook some less than ideal behavior on the part of the host or hostess (or of some of the guests).

If Party Is Given for Boys Instead of Girls

For boys, this party should be somewhat less complex. Following a complicated spider web or making complicated things might be a little hard for boys. They can make simple things instead—if the party has an Indian theme, for instance, they can make Indian hats.

Spider, if simplified, would be all right for boys. Clues would be all right. But remember that boys move around more, need a chance to be physically active and boisterous. Boys do not have party manners as some girls do. Parties for boys need to go faster. Boys need to move from one activity to another more rapidly than do girls.

Six to Eleven

It is the novelty, the excitement of a new experience, that makes a party such a happy and welcome occasion for the child in these middle years from six through eleven. He is now losing, or has already lost, his preschool self-consciousness that made it hard for him to participate. In those younger years children seem to need many props to make a party a success, and most of all they need the simple and the familiar.

The preschooler can talk a great deal about parties, but he is often more involved in the idea and the trappings surrounding the party than in the party itself. Party clothes, which he will repudiate in these middle years, were earlier an important part of the party. And often the cake *was* the party. But when party time actually came, all too frequently the excitement of anticipation produced a stomach upset, or the unfamiliarity of the scene made the child either freeze on the spot or explode in wild abandon.

But by these middle years "the party's the thing," and the child is ready to lose himself in it, or at least to participate fully. The intensity of the moment that is the party is so charged that it is enjoyed at the moment and well remembered. Children in these middle years live with the memory of their last party, in the midst of planning for their next, a year apart. For "party" in these years almost always means "birthday party." It is not until ten or eleven that either the significance of age palls, or the importance of other events such as special holidays might provide an impetus stronger than "birthday" for the giving of a party.

The child in these years not only enjoys taking part in his party, but he wants to help his parents in the planning. He usually knows whether he wants just boys or girls or both. He can, however, be influenced by his mother in the younger years of six to eight. Mothers often choose a one-sex party, especially at six, when they feel it may be less hectic. Boys on the whole are more prone to choose just boys, and by nine and ten years of age one-sex parties predominate. The planned activity can be more easily geared to the interest of one sex. Thus a Fashion-party for 7-year-olds may be thought of more strictly as a girls' party, though there are a selected few boys who might long to be invited. (After all, leading fashion designers are very often men!) Conversely, a Pirate-party at ten might be restricted to boys. (But think of those special girls who resist dresses and who prefer to play with boys who might be a real addition to such a party.)

Perhaps most important of all is that a parent needs to be selective (though not too exclusive) in planning the guest list. Since it is at six and seven that children may feel most excluded, parents need to think around the situation, so that other activities can be planned later for those neighbors or friends who may have to be left out; or maybe even a duplicate party could be given. But holding the number of guests close to the child's age is important; it can act as a check to prevent parties from growing too large, and can sometimes serve as an excuse for limiting the guest list. The inclusion of younger siblings can at times disrupt a party. The wise parent will plan some enticing activity away from home to happily engage younger siblings.

Parents soon learn the kinds of activities which different age children enjoy. They also learn all too soon the speed with which younger children race through activities, leaving the hapless parent quite breathless and wondering what to do next. Planning for extra activities (which can be held in reserve) allays the anxiety of the parent, even if these extra activities don't actually need to be used.

Though well-planned activities can keep the party flowing smoothly, the high spirits of children in this age range can mount to real bedlam ending with wrestling and silliness. A certain amount of this must be expected, especially with boys. But the adults in charge may need to exert firm control, especially with 6- to 8-year-olds. This is why a number of adults need to be on hand.

Often the best insurance for keeping a party from going to pieces is to plan it with enough variety so that out-of-bounds or destructive forces won't have a chance to materialize. A shift to a museum, animal farm, or bowling alley can be an organizing force, especially for the 6- to 8-year-old. Nine- and 10-year-olds are more controlled in themselves and thrive on a well-planned party that will exercise their skills. And they are as good at watching others as at acting themselves, for even in watching and cheering teammates they are participating as a part of a team. They do not need to go afield as do children who are slightly younger.

By eleven a transitional stage is reached which often makes this a less favorable party age. The best control at this age, if you do have a party, is to keep the sexes separated. This usually pleases the boys, though many girls, pushing into the interests of the years to come, want parties with boys. Unless these are well controlled, as in a dancing-school situation, boy-girl parties at eleven usually are not very successful. It would be far better for the girls to give up the thought of a party if they cannot be happy in each other's company. Boys, with their vigorous athletic urges, structure an all-boy party more readily. And their bull-session type of humor and enjoyment can while away party time, all in the midst of their acting like a litter of puppies.

SIX

The 6-year-old characteristically wants to be first, to be loved most, to receive the exclusive attention of any adult who may be present. He finds it most difficult to wait while anybody else is having a turn. All of this makes him less than an ideal party guest.

The 6-year-old is often at his worst with his own mother. Cheerful, enthusiastic, co-operative though he may occasionally be with others, he tends to be quarrelsome, demanding, exacting with his own mother, or in her presence. Tears and tantrums take place most often when she is present. Thus any 6-year-old party will proceed more smoothly when the guests' mothers are not on hand.

SIX not only wants, he seems to need, always to win. Thus multiple prize-giving is necessary at a 6-year-old party to keep everybody happy. This multiple giving of prizes, especially of a farewell gift for each child, is also important because of the fact that SIX is characteristically more of a taker than a giver. Though it is not difficult for the 6-year-old to give a gift to the birthday child, he feels like a birthday child himself and wants a present in return. If he himself receives a certain amount of party loot, it will make things easier and more satisfactory for him.

SIX is by nature combative and aggressively quarrelsome. When differences of opinion arise in his play with friends, he is prone to "fight it out" in overt, physical combat. Thus, constant adult supervision is needed to maintain harmony.

SIX's emotions are violent and uncontrolled. SIXES at a party can easily disintegrate either into silly laughter or into hysterical tears. Thus adults in charge will need to be on their toes every minute to prevent chaos.

But—the 6-year-old *loves* a party. He anticipates it in advance, relishes it while it lasts, and enjoys it in retrospect. Thus, most parents do find the whole venture worth while because of the pleasure it gives, in spite of temperamental difficulties which tend to make a party for 6-year-olds hazardous and exhausting for the adults in charge.

Warming up

Opening the presents

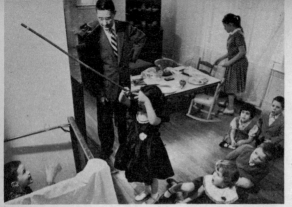

Fish pond

Hot potato

High spirits

Top: Finding places

Center: The party under way

Right: "What did you get?"

SIX-YEAR-OLD PARTY

Key

As at five, the key to success here is good advance planning. However, the planning should include the realization that the schedule may not be followed as rigidly as seemed desirable at five. Definite planned activity is important at the beginning and end of this party, but other plans may need to shift as the party proceeds.

NUMBER OF GUESTS: Five guests (plus host or hostess) make an ideal number. Both boys and girls may be included.

NUMBER OF ADULTS: Adults at the party should be Mother, Father, and one adult helper; or Mother and two adult helpers. No parents of guests stay—parents bring the children and drop them just outside the house. Most SIXES behave much better when their mothers are not there.

Schedule

Party hours will depend on whether party is held on a weekend day or on a school day. On a weekend, a lunch party is good—from 1 to 3 P.M. If the party has to be on a school day, it might be held from 3:30 to 5:30. Two hours is long enough.

1:00–1:20 Definite planned activity here is important, but it has to be individual, since all will not arrive at the same time. Children sit at a small table and color, cut, play with pipe cleaners or Plasticine. Host opens presents during this period, and guests watch. But this may not be too orderly. Some hosts will wait till all presents have arrived; others prefer not to. Some may refuse to open presents at this time.

1:20–1:30 Children play games—the same games which they play and like at school. (Find this out from your child in advance.) Good games are Doggie Doggie Where's Your Bone; Hot Potato; Giant Step.

1:30–2:00 Refreshments. Table as at other ages has been set beforehand and is ready in another room. A simple luncheon menu may include carrot sticks, hot dogs and rolls, cake, ice cream, milk. At each place are a paper plate, heavy small glass, napkin, big place card with name lettered in big capital letters, since now most can read their own names and like to do so. There can be a little paper cup at each place with candy in it. Favors—ring, penny, button, thimble, each wrapped in wax paper—may be in the cake. A homemade party hat for each child can be a big feature of the luncheon. There is lots of eating, lots of talk, much interest in hats, in favors, and in each other.

2:00–2:10 Fishing Pond game. Behind a sheet-draped card table, representing the pond, one of the adults or an older sibling sits and puts little presents onto hooks dangled from fishing poles. Children take turns. Suitable gifts for this are: Scotch tape, little pencil sharpeners of special shapes, tape measures, Life Savers, little Indian figures.

2:10–end Some kind of outing if weather permits. The length of this will vary some, depending on the kind of outing and the distance to be traveled, so the party might need to last a little longer than the prescribed two hours.

Good places to visit on such an outing include: museum, animal farm, nature center, zoo, toy-train exhibit. The three adults take the children in two cars. When this trip is over, give each child a final farewell present (as for instance a little live turtle) and drop him off at his home.

(If anything happens, as it may, so that you cannot go on this trip, a good substitute activity is a cartoon movie shown at home. In fact, if a projector and film need to be hired,* it may be safer to have them on hand anyway. . . . If your planned trip seems to be falling through and you cannot obtain a film and projector, you might fill in this final period by letting the children watch a suitable TV program.)

Expenses

This is a fairly expensive party, with favors, gifts, expense of renting projector and film. It might cost as much as $15.

Hints and Warnings

Allow some flexibility of schedule but do not allow the children to take over, or things will become a shambles.

This will probably be a very wearing party for the adults in charge.

* Film and projector can usually be rented from a local optical store or from your local YMCA.

Six-year-olds often act very badly at parties. They can go wild more quickly than children of almost any other age. They tend to do this in a destructive, noisy way. They may pinch, poke, push, fight. Their humor is apt to be aggressive. Their drive toward activity and exploration is tremendous. They are likely to get out-of-bounds unless well supervised. Their emotions are strong and not well controlled. Don't be surprised if there are tears and trouble. Considerable organization and control on the part of the adult are necessary.

The 6-year-old is extremely acquisitive, very egocentric, and a great collector. He may want everything for himself. Other people's things may get into the bag in which he is collecting his toys and favors. Also, host or guests may behave in a self-centered, demanding, unmannerly way not usually considered suitable by adults for either hosts or guests. Solve problems as simply as possible.

SEVEN

Seven is one of those seemingly inconsistent ages when the child, though he may be having considerable trouble within himself, does not make much trouble for those around him. It is frequently the case that at exuberant, outgoing, aggressive ages, such as four and six, children are very hard to get along with but they themselves may not suffer too much because of their own behavior. At the more withdrawn ages, such as seven, they may give relatively little trouble to others, even though they themselves may be uncertain and unhappy.

Especially do we find SEVEN easy to get along with in a positive social situation such as a party with friends. He may complain before and after the event, but his behavior during a party is often remarkably good. And the control of this age (which may lead to moping, complaining, and even sulking at home) seems to help the 7-year-old, much more so than the 6- and 8-year-old, to be reasonably restrained and amenable in an outside social situation. Less egocentric and aggressive than SIX, less wild than EIGHT, he seems to enjoy taking his part in group activity.

He does not always have to be first and to win as he did just earlier. He not only can take his turn but enjoys the notion of turns. He also likes the idea of having and obeying rules. However, much less exacting and demanding than he will be later, he is not disturbed by moderate infractions of these rules. Thus, his behavior can be modified and to some extent governed by the idea of rules, but he does not insist on strict adherence to them, to the extent of interfering with a party.

However, the 7-year-old is not a good judge of his own stamina. SEVENS in a party situation as elsewhere are given to a somewhat reckless expenditure of energy till suddenly they drop from fatigue. Keeping the party hours brief can prevent this complication.

SEVEN is somewhat serial-minded. He is poor at terminations. Thus it is important to shift quickly from one game to another so that the group will not get "stuck" and go on and on with the same activity till it palls and behavior deteriorates.

Also, though SEVEN likes the idea of rules, he cannot follow too-complicated instructions. Thus, a quick series of relatively simple games is better for him than a few complicated activities.

SEVEN-YEAR-OLD PARTY

Key

This is an easy age for party-giving because children are at seven fascinated by the idea of following rules even though they may not carry them out perfectly.

NUMBER OF GUESTS: Six to eight is a good number of guests for a 7-year-old party. Both boys and girls may be invited, though some prefer to invite just boys or just girls. Girls may not mind too much either way, but many boys prefer just boys.

NUMBER OF ADULTS: Two adults can manage a party at this age—the mother and one helper.

Schedule

From 3:30 to 5:00 is a good time for such a party. One and a half hours is actually better than two. Many become too tired and too excited if the party lasts longer than this, perhaps because their increasing speed takes them through so many games.

3:30–3:50   Children will enjoy Bingo while waiting for all to assemble. This is a quiet game; they work together; it gets them acquainted if necessary; the number of guests doesn't matter; and children of this age like working with numbers.

3:50–4:00   Peanut Hunt. (Gum may be hidden as well as peanuts.)

4:00–4:15   Refreshments. SEVENS need a mid-afternoon snack, and having the refreshments early gives them the energy to keep going without becoming too cross, hungry, and tired. Refreshments consist of simple sandwiches, ice cream, cake, milk. Children at this age tend to approach the refreshments with great enthusiasm, but fill up quickly and get up from the table quickly. If balloons are used for decoration, as they may well be, children may start hitting them and pulling them down. They are allowed to do this, though preferably after eating.

4:15–5:00   A series of games follows, all at one level—just game after game, for the rest of the available time. This rather than having large blocks of activity as at six and at eight years. Simple relay games, boys against the girls, are especially popular. Other possible games include: Musical Chairs, Ring Toss, Pin the Tail on the Donkey or seasonal variations (as Nose on Snowman, Hat on Scarecrow).

          Prizes are given to the winner or winners of each game. Suitable prizes include: trading cards, paper dolls, toy jewelry—as Poppets—doll-house furniture, false mustaches or noses, chewing gum, Life Savers.

5:00   Ending of party and getting guests home. Children can play games right up to the time for termination; then the host's mother takes them home. This gets them out of the house, and prevents the confusion which often accompanies parents' arrival. It also saves waiting for the parents to arrive. (Since eating early has allowed the adult helper to clear away the table and remnants of the food, things will be in reasonably good shape when the mother returns home in time to get dinner.)

38

Expenses

Prizes, gum, peanuts will cost around $5. Refreshments around $5. Thus the total should come to around $10.

Hints and Warnings

This is an age when chicken pox and other communicable diseases, as well as accidents to arms and legs, may cut down the guest list, so prepare for last-minute replacements.

Some are apt to be very silly at this age. SEVENS love to clown, so some clowning should be allowed. It is fairly easy to control. However, behavior is apt to deteriorate into shapelessness unless games follow each other rapidly. All games should be well planned in advance and all equipment ready.

At six and at eight it seems to work out best to plan for large blocks of activity. At seven, games can simply follow each other. A party at this age can be very simple, more so than at many other ages. The main thing seems to be to have plenty of games, and to have all details and equipment ready.

Don't insist too much on strict carrying out of rules. Children like rules at this age and like to think they are carrying them out, but actually they do not mind minor infractions. Turns and order are important, but they do not care about strict adherence to the details of rules. If infractions bother *them*, then that is the time to step in. If they are bothered they will clamor, "That's not fair!" Otherwise, don't be too strict. In lining up, children are able to decide among themselves the order. Also they can usually decide about turns—"I'm first!" The more pushy ones get to be first, but this doesn't seem to do much harm, except perhaps to the adult sense of fairness.

SEVENS seem to hold up well for about one and one-half hours; then they are apt to go to pieces. Thus the party should not last too long.

Have the party in as indestructible a setting as possible. Children will push, jump, scuffle, knock things over. A basement or playroom setting is good if available.

As at six, it is important to have paper bags marked with children's names, for their loot; also a good safe place where they can put these bags, so they won't worry that somebody else is getting their things. Be sure that each child gets at least one prize, even if he or she doesn't actually win anything. In fact, frequent prize-giving to all is a good plan.

39

Seven-Year-Old Party

SEVENS tend to move as a group. When one does something, the others are likely to follow. A little adult direction is often needed to keep things from getting too far out of hand.

This 7-year-old party as described may sound rather simple and unpretentious, but that seems to be, at least in our experience, the way that SEVENS like it.

Alternative Suggestions

A variation of the more usual 7-year-old party at home might be a short Theater Party, if for example a puppet show, ballet, or some special children's performance were available. The refreshment part of such a party would best precede the theater. Then the children can be delivered directly to their homes once the theater entertainment is over.

A Cooking Party is a special treat for 7-year-old girls. Guests can prepare part of the menu during the party. Cookie dough could be prepared ahead of time, ready to roll out. Interesting cookie cutters can be provided. The party mother will need to help with timing of oven baking, etc., without interfering with the spontaneous fun of the party. Provision of pretty colored toppings for the cookies adds to the enjoyment. The guests could also make their own beverage—some form of nectar drink. It is surprising to see how pleased and impressed 7-year-olds can be with participation in such a seemingly simple project as combining nectar powder, sugar, water, and ice cubes. The tasting, stirring, and general discussion all add to the fun.

SEVENS, especially girls, still enjoy dressing up, and enter into a Fashion Party with a certain amount of abandon. All that is needed is the provision of "dress-up" clothes: skirts, fancy scarves, hats, shoes, gloves, purses, jewelry, make-up, facial tissue, and cotton puffs. Plenty of space and, if possible, several full-length mirrors for primping and viewing themselves provide a good setting.

EIGHT

Expansive! Speedy! Evaluative! Thus we have, in past publications, described the 8-year-old. All of these qualities have their advantages. But any of them can be a handicap when it comes to a party, unless taken into account in the party planning.

Expansive EIGHT looks for new fields to conquer—and to enjoy! Thus, ideally, a party for 8-year-olds will extend beyond the confines of the host or hostess' home to include a trip to a nearby bowling alley or miniature golf range. And even within the home, some new and unusual area of entertainment such as a magician's act might successfully be offered.

Speedy EIGHT will run through quite a lot of entertainment in a short space of time. No single activity should last overlong, and a good supply of different activities must be provided.

Evaluative EIGHT is less easily pleased than when he was younger. For this reason it is important to provide entertainment of a fairly high quality. EIGHT is skeptical as well as evaluative. Thus it might be better to have no magic act at all rather than an unskilled one. (However, a really skilled 13–15-year-old magician may be more highly appreciated and more fun than a polished adult magician.)

EIGHT's well-known enjoyment and enthusiasm make him an ideal candidate as a party guest. The very same qualities, however, can make him a real menace at a party unless it is carefully planned, speedily conducted, and fully supervised. A houseful of roughhousing 8-year-old boys has caused many a mother to vow, "Never again!" after her son's guests, and her son, have turned the house into a shambles.

But, as we say, the warmth, enjoyment, and full appreciation which 8-year-olds feel, and enthusiastically express at the end of an 8-year-old party which has been skillfully planned and conducted with their good traits, and limitations, in mind, make it evident that contrary to popular belief, eight can be an ideal age for a party.

EIGHT-YEAR-OLD PARTY

Key

Planned entertainment, with alternating quiet and boisterous or active periods, is the secret of success at this age. Large blocks of activity fill up the time happily and avoid bedlam.

NUMBER OF GUESTS: Six to eight guests is a good number, all girls or all boys. As at seven, you could probably successfully have both boys and girls. Boys, however, may be very definite about preferring "no girls!"

NUMBER OF ADULTS: Three adults are needed for this party—father, mother, helper with car.

Schedule

The best hours for a party at this age are from 4 to 6, dinner included.

4:00–5:00 Some planned away-from-home activity. Take them to this right away as soon as three or four have gathered. (Comic books may be read if there is any waiting.) Activities could be bowling at a bowling alley, miniature golf, hitting golf balls at a driving range. No prizes are needed.

5:00–5:30 Magician or other activity at home.

5:30–6:00   Refreshments. Choice of hamburgers or hot dogs, buns, raw carrots, potato chips, peanuts, milk (to be drunk through straws), ice cream or popsicles, cake. Table favors can be puzzle rings (ball and groove), so that children can play with them or swap them right at the table. Table conversation flows quite naturally but may at times need to be stimulated by adults. Decorations are not particularly necessary.

6:00   Party ends at the table. This is not too dangerous, as they do not feel too wild after eating, so that planned activity need not be arranged for this period of parting. Some parents will call for their children; some guests can probably walk home alone. Any who have to wait could watch TV.

Expenses

Expense could be a problem. Bowling (or other initial outside activity) would probably cost around $2.50, but might be more. Refreshments might be around $6. Magician would be the most expensive item, probably varying from $5 to $15, unless you have a friend who can do *good* magic tricks.

Hints and Warnings

An 8-year-old party, especially a party for boys, can turn into real bedlam unless planned and supervised carefully. Eight-year-olds are physically very wild and boisterous. So plan every minute! And furthermore, plan what to do if they come early. Guests may arrive anywhere from an hour to a week early, so plan accordingly! Also, if the magician is late, have a substitute activity planned. (Have all games planned carefully, as well, with all equipment ready.)

Good games to be played if there is any time to be filled in are ball games, play with electric trains, wrestling on mats.

As to the magician: it is better to have no magician at all than a poor one. EIGHTS are very skeptical and very critical. It works best for the magician to do quiet (but clever) things first to get the children's co-operation and to win over their initial skepticism. Children are not primarily impressed with technical ability, but they do love to assist a magician. And as magician Theo Doré, of New York, has commented, "They are more impressed when the magician finds fifty-cent pieces behind their friends' ears than they would be if he produced a live elephant from a small box." If you cannot afford the magician or cannot get

43

one, fill in the time with planned games. You can try contacting your local schools, however, to see if they may be able to provide a good teen-age magician.

Activities should not last too long. Bowling should be no more than forty-five minutes; magician's act should not last for more than half an hour.

With EIGHTS, the main problem is at the beginning of the party. They tend to relax as the party goes on, and usually they want to please the adult by the end of the party—particularly if they are having a good time. As they leave, EIGHTS often make very warm comments, such as, "This was the most thrilling experience of my life."

Unlike the 7-year-old party, which involves quite a series of different games, the 8-year-old party involves merely several large blocks of time, each filled with a single kind of more elaborate activity.

Presents and prizes for guests are not essential at this age.

If Party Is Given for Girls Instead of Boys

Actually you would have very much this same kind of party for girls. The chief difference is that the girls are not as much of a menace at a party at this age as are boys. They tend to become silly, but are not so rough. Girls as well as boys will enjoy bowling.

NINE

Nine is not a sure-fire age for a party. Most 10-year-olds are
friendly, appreciative, and quite easily pleased with the adult's
efforts to entertain them, but not so with NINES, who have very
definite likes and dislikes and do not bother to conceal them.
Some things thrill them, others bore them, and they make this
quite evident. Nor do they resemble 8-year-olds, who may them-

45

selves have a good time at a party even when their behavior is too boisterous to be satisfactory to the adults in charge.

Thus, it behooves the adult who is giving a party for children of this age to keep in mind the outstanding characteristics of the age. If he does not, even quite strenuous efforts may go for nothing, since NINE is far less easily entertained, his imagination less easily caught, than earlier. Play activities need really to be interesting and somewhat unusual if NINES are going to have a good time.

Here are some of the outstanding characteristics of the age, knowledge of which will help considerably in the successful planning of a 9-year-old party.

First of all, NINES love to compete and they love to show off their (often not inconsiderable) skills. Thus, competitive games involving a display of real skills are strongly recommended.

Nine-year-olds are real traders at heart. Thus, a party should ideally provide both objects and opportunity for some trading to take place.

Furthermore, most NINES have an abundance of physical energy. Thus they enjoy, and even need, plenty of games which allow them to expend this energy, and ample space (preferably outdoor space) in which to expend it.

Nine-year-olds are still young enough for their behavior, especially in boys, to deteriorate quickly to sheer physical rough-housing, if they are bored, overstimulated, or inadequately supervised. Careful planning, organization, timing, and supervision by strong, capable adults are therefore important.

Cowgirls arrive

Branding

Top right: Calf roping

Top left: Wild horse race

Beware of rattlesnakes

Treasure hunt

Bronco riders' relay

Top: Filling the trough

Center: Bread and jelly relay

Bottom: Ring toss

"Come and get it!"

Siesta

Favors

Opening the presents

NINE-YEAR-OLD PARTY

Key

The key to success here, even more than at other ages, is that there should be the most minute preplanning. Such planning avoids two opposite dangers. NINES easily either get out of hand or experience extreme boredom. Either of these can ruin a party. Parties at this age need to use up the tremendous energy of the child and also to offer a constant challenge. The most effective activity is a series of relay games in which either individuals, or two teams, compete. Some central theme, such as a Wild West or Pirate theme, both stimulates the children's imaginations and helps to organize and unify the party.

NUMBER OF GUESTS: Because of the competitive team activities, it is important to have an even number of children. Nine guests (plus host or hostess) is a good number.

NUMBER OF ADULTS: Mother and one or two adult helpers, and possibly an older sibling.

Schedule*

A middle-of-the-day party is good, perhaps from noon till 3 P.M.

12:00–12:10 Children have been instructed to wear clothing appropriate to the theme of the party. No costumes to be bought— rather, they wear jeans and sweaters or jackets. (Adults as well as children are dressed in this style.) Guests are left by their parents near the yard or grounds, not brought to the door. A sign at the entrance of the yard can indicate that this is the D.Y. (or whatever the child's initials are) RANCH. Guests are at once "branded" with the ranch brand (adhesive tape stuck onto their jeans).

12:10–12:20 Treasure hunt, called "The Roundup." Appropriate "treasures"—such as sheriffs' badge, horseshoe nail, arrow, bandanna, saddle blanket, rope, small figure of a cow, wagon wheel—are hidden about the yard.

* We are, for the sake of specificity, describing a Wild West party, and are giving schedule and details for this sort of party. If some different theme is chosen, you will need to do your careful planning along the lines indicated here, but making up your own schedule and details.

12:20–12:50   A series of competitive games involving individual skills. Good games include the following: Calf Roping, which consists of riding a three-foot stick horse, and at the same time kicking a rubber ball toward (and eventually into) a paper bag anchored at the end of a twenty-foot path. Each contestant is timed. Filling the Trough is played by having the contestants run with a narrow-necked bottle filled with water which they empty into a saucepan. This, too, is timed.

12:50–1:20   Casual lunch, possibly served from a chuck wagon improvised from a regular express wagon covered as if it were a covered wagon. Lunch consists of sandwiches in paper bags, which can be taken into the house and eaten. (Living room has been transformed into a ranch house by pushing back the furniture and spreading blankets before the fire.) Cocoa can be served from a large coffeepot. Cowboy records or someone playing a guitar furnish a musical background. Guests may at first listen and then later join in singing.

1:20–1:40   Quiet activities indoors. Sample game is Horse and Rider, in which girls while blindfolded draw, on paper, a horse. They take their hands off the paper and then, still blindfolded, draw a rider.

1:40–2:25   Team relay games, out of doors. This can be a series of team relays, each relay being given a different cowboy-type name. In Wild Horse Race, for instance, each person rides a stick horse to a given goal and back again to her team. In Beware of Rattlesnakes, children run, or again ride a stick horse, between balloons which are scattered between two parallel strings. The purpose is to jump over the balloons without breaking them. Bronco Riders' Relay is a variety of leapfrog. One child rushes ahead and crouches on the ground, and another runs and jumps over her. Then she crouches and the next girl jumps over her, till the goal is reached.

2:25–2:35   Guests may at this point wish to rest briefly. In fact, they may collapse, worn out by team games.

2:35–3:00   Guests return indoors for the awarding of prizes—prizes for both individual and for team games; for the giving of favors; and for the eating of birthday cake and ice cream.

Expenses

Main expenses are for prizes, favors, refreshments. Prizes and favors (including objects for the treasure hunt) might be kept down to around $6, though they might cost a good deal more. Refreshments are around $7.

Hints and Warnings

This is one of the hardest parties to give because it requires so much planning and so much supervision. But it can, if successful, be one of the most rewarding, because children of this age enjoy a good party so much and express their enjoyment so openly and freely. However, remember that the most detailed planning is necessary. Otherwise guests may wrestle, read comic books, or simply sit around being bored.

Since good weather is virtually essential for this party, the party may need to be postponed until a clear day—sometimes even more than once. Fortunately, most NINES can accept this delay and disappointment.

Since competition and the wish to win are strong at this age, the make-up of the relay teams should be frequently changed. Otherwise a poor contestant might continually obstruct the progress of one team.

Adults can join in when needed—if, for instance, pairs of contestants are needed.

This is a great age for trading. Guests may want to trade not only prizes and favors but even their sandwiches. Thus, there should be a variety in kinds of sandwiches available.

Prizes are important at this age, as earlier. However, since there is so much pleasure at this age simply in achieving or in winning, the actual prize-giving can be postponed until the end of the party, and all prizes given at once. (This may be the first age when bags for collecting "loot" are not necessary.)

Good prizes (prizes may be selected by the winners, in turn, from a tray) include: Scotch tape, little notebooks, combs, toy white mice. Prize winners may be determined as follows: each winner of an individual competition, and each member of any winning team, receives a stamp mark on the back of her hand. Total number of marks received can determine first, second, third and booby prize winners. Favors may include: china horses, gilt-covered chocolate coins (for money bags), etc.

If Party Is Given for Boys Instead of Girls

Roughly the same plan may be followed if the party is given for boys instead of for girls. However, boys are more likely to get into wrestling or roughhousing in a tightly organized party, or when refreshments are eaten indoors. Thus, more widespread outdoor activity will need to be provided. The treasure hunt could be expanded; they might for instance dig for treasure.

Boys particularly like to show off any skills they may have, in competition. Thus, some activities, such as those appropriate to an Olympic Games theme, could be introduced into the program. Also, boys of this age like very much to make things from models. Thus, models of objects which would fit into the theme of the party (covered wagons for instance, if available) could be provided, and boys could make these.

TEN

Ten, like five, is frequently referred to as a Golden Age, and this holds as true for TEN in a party situation as in any other. The ordinary 10-year-old is an easy person to entertain because his demands are few and easily satisfied, his appreciation is warm and readily expressed, his critical ability is limited, his natural, easygoing friendliness is extended to children and adults alike. With adults he is old enough to be responsive, without being old enough to criticize the adult or to resent his presence. With other children, he is friendly and uncritical and does not yet feel the need to "boss" and direct the others, which will come in at eleven.

Thus, TENS at a party are fun to entertain, since they are enthusiastic rather than boisterous, appreciative rather than critical, contributing rather than demanding. They get on well with other guests, co-operating fully in games; are quick to appreciate and to remark favorably about decoration, costumes worn by others, prizes. They come to a party to enjoy themselves, and usually succeed in doing so.

Self-criticism, like criticism of others, is largely absent at this age. Thus they can enter fully and without embarrassment or shyness into any activity suggested. Most children at this age like to follow rules and are reasonably able to do so—thus games with rules usually go well.

For the most part, TENS do not impose their wishes, likes, interests on a party as do 9-year-olds. Rather they come to a party with an enthusiastic interest and a positive readiness to take part in whatever may be offered.

Girls and boys together are not at their best at ten, and, for this reason, parties for one sex only usually work out best.

Ten is known as a balanced age. "Maybe—maybe not," he answers questions put to him. "Sometimes I do—sometimes I don't." Thus he is ready to go in either, or any, direction and can easily fit into almost any reasonable entertainment which may be offered.

Many 10-year-olds are not primarily interested in celebrating their birthdays with a party. However, they may rise very nicely to some party for a special occasion such as Halloween, Valentine's Day, St. Patrick's Day. While such parties are suitable for other ages as well, they seem to be especially suitable at ten.

TEN-YEAR-OLD PARTY

Key

Since most 10-year-olds tend to be friendly, easygoing, well-adjusted, and uncritical, giving a party at this age should not be difficult. It is not as demanding of adults as at other ages. The actual format of the party is not too important, but children of this age especially enjoy a party built around some special holiday theme. The party we describe is a Halloween party, for girls only.

NUMBER OF GUESTS: It is probably best to have party guests all of the same sex. The exact number doesn't matter—six to ten is a good number.

NUMBER OF ADULTS: The mother can manage alone, but things will go more smoothly if there is one helper.

Schedule

A supper party is a good idea. This works out especially well for Halloween, since a party timed from 5:30 to 7:00 allows guests to go out Halloweening from 7:00 to 8:00. The exact timing of events does not matter, since one game or event can follow another rather fluidly. The important thing is to start supper in time to get through by 7:00 as all guests will be impatient to get out into the night.

5:30–5:40   Filling in the time till all guests have arrived is not difficult at this age and does not have to be planned for. Guests arrive in costume: Gravel Gertie, Geisha girl, pony, Raggedy Ann doll, etc. The hostess's mother may also wear a simple costume. Each girl has a mask but does not wear it in the house. Children at this age tend to be extremely enthusiastic and uncritical about each other's costumes: "Oh, that's adorable!" Guests are pleased with and unself-conscious about their own costumes.

5:40–5:50   Bobbing for Apples. Provide a pan of water with apples in it. Apples should have good stems. Towel should be available for wiping faces. Each guest is allowed four (rather protracted) trials to grasp an apple with her teeth—hands behind her. A small group is best for this so that all can cluster around, see what is going on, and not wait too long for turns.

Doughnut on String—hanging in doorway. This too is to be attacked only with the mouth, hands not used. Two at a time allows for a contest. This can be started while some are still ducking for apples.

5:50–6:00   Pan of flour with ring hidden in it. Place a shallow pan on a small table. A ring is hidden in the flour, which is one-half to three-fourth inch deep. Each girl can make two cuts with a knife. If she uncovers, or partially uncovers the ring, then she may try to get it with her teeth. A towel is necessary to wipe flour from faces. A prize is given to anyone getting the ring in her teeth. Only one chance is given.

6:00–6:20   Chamber of Horrors. All lights are turned off and girls sit in a circle. Hostess tells some gruesome story, ending with the hero getting killed. Then she says she has saved a few souvenirs to remember him by. (These souvenirs are on the table beside her or just outside the door.) She passes them around, one at a time. Souvenirs may include:

> The murdered man's hair (head of a mop)
> His eyes (grapes)
> His intestines (cooked spaghetti)
> His teeth (chalk)
> His ears (potato chips)

If supper is not ready by this time, the guests may take turns telling ghost stories.

6:20–7:00 Supper by Candlelight. The table is set in the dining room with Halloween paper tablecloth, napkins, paper cups, plates. Decorations may include centerpiece of pumpkins with candles and little wax figures made in Halloween shapes at each place. Dining room may be further decorated, if the hostess wishes, with crepe-paper streamers, skeletons pinned to curtains, etc. Halloween colored "blowers" may be provided at each place. The menu may include hamburgers, cole slaw, rolls, cocoa with marshmallows, relish, and cookies and ice cream for dessert. The beginning of 11- to 12-year-old clowning with food may be seen even here, as some may use cole slaw for false teeth, etc., but this fooling is not excessive.

As initial hunger is calmed down, guests may start on ghost stories again. However, the stories are likely to deteriorate at this point to rude remarks, or blowing of blowers as guests wait for "seconds."

7:00 Mother provides Halloween "Trick or Treat" bags for each and gives directions as to where they may and may not go. She tells guests to check back at 8 o'clock, or else to go directly home if they live near enough.

Expenses

This is not an expensive party. Twelve dollars should cover the entire cost, including food and decorations, provided decorations and favors are not too elaborate.

Ten-Year-Old Party

Hints and Warnings

At this age, a Halloween or any other holiday party requires good (though not necessarily expensive) decorations. For a Halloween party, a pasteboard skeleton can hang in front of the doorway through which guests enter. Black cats and Halloween figures can be fastened to the fireplace or curtains, and can stand on the mantel. Streamers may be used. Lighted pumpkins may be placed outside the front door.

For the party described, just a few pieces of equipment are needed, but they should be, as at other ages, all assembled beforehand (with some kept out of sight until needed). They include: kettle or dishpan of water with apples for bobbing; plate with flour, ring hidden in it, knife beside it, placed on newspaper or piece of Halloween paper on a magazine or luggage stand; towels for wiping off faces; doughnuts suspended by a string from doorway; grapes, spaghetti, etc. for parts of dead man, available on a small table. . . . Good prizes include noisemakers, or "pirate gold"—chocolate candy covered with gilt paper in sacks.

Though one mother actually could manage this party alone, a helper is useful, especially at the beginning when more than one game is going on. At this age, guests tend to be quite insistent that rules be carried out by others, even though they may "cheat" a little themselves. Things move along more rapidly and effectively if there is adequate supervision. Ten-year-olds like to follow rules (for the most part) and like to have rules followed by others, but need a little help in seeing that things go in an orderly fashion.

This party emphasizes oral activities. If there is a good deal of flu around or if colds are prevalent among the guests, more hygienic activities should be substituted for those described here. Or Doughnut on String could be omitted, even if others are kept.

Girl guests at a party like this tend to be rather noisy and active. (Boys may of course be even noisier and more active.) But as a rule children of either sex, at ten, are reasonably docile and easy to supervise, even though enthusiastic and noisy.

Since guests are anxious to get through eating and get outdoors, the dessert which ends the meal should be simple and easy to eat. If time is running out, ice cream can be omitted and cookies—which can be eaten on the run—may provide the sole dessert.

For the Horror Story, it is best to have the girls sitting in a circle, and not too far apart, so that they can easily pass things. Though the table with the "horrors" on it can be set just outside the door, it helps to have it right in the room beside the storyteller, who can identify the various objects she wants to pass by the aid of a small pencil flashlight.

This is an especially good age to omit younger siblings, if possible. Children younger than ten sometimes do not mind if siblings get in the way and interfere with the orderliness of the various procedures. But TENS like order, and siblings often make it difficult to carry out the various games. Particularly do they get in the way during the telling of the Horror Story. If possible, it is desirable to have younger members of the family doing their Halloweening at someone else's house.

(Halloween is an excellent time to have a party for the child of any age. The decorations and costumes come naturally. The very nature of the occasion and the fact of being in costume tend to put guests into a receptive, holiday mood. The fact that they are looking forward to going out for "Trick or Treating" lends a point and excitement to all the activities which precede, and lessens the demand that the party itself be the focal point of excitement. Guests' demands on a party such as this tend to be small. They need some games, conducted in a more or less orderly fashion, something scary, and, of course, food.)

Alternative Suggestions

With TEN's love of old clothes and his abhorrence of dressing up, a Hobo Party could be quite to his liking for either indoor or outdoor activities. Guests could come in patched or ragged jeans and shirts, battered hats, etc. TEN's growing interest in geography and his special delight in spot geography, as for instance in locating cities on a map, could lead to the selection of a Hobo Hike as a featured activity. A large map of the United States can be hung on the wall, with ten to fifteen cities numbered in order and encircled. Letters such as Anagram or Scrabble squares are drawn one at a time out of a large container—a hat or basket. A child may move from one city to the next if he draws a letter in his first (or last) name. He moves by tracing a line from one city to the next with a colored crayon, each child having his own specific color. All sit on the floor awaiting their chance to hobo across the United States. The first person to reach the farthest destination wins the prize.

Other competitive games can be similar to those described for the 9-year-old party. Refreshments could center around a cook-out or fireplace. A large kettle of baked beans or chili could provide the main dish, along with hot rolls. A hot or cold beverage could be served in mugs.

A Pirate Party may be especially designed for 10-year-old boys. They can come in appropriate costumes. The provision of eye patches after they get to the party, along with drawing of tattoos on their hands and arms, will add to the realism of their roles. Walking the plank (onto a mattress), singing pirate songs, hunting for buried treasure (actually buried) with the aid of a pirate's map can be exciting parts of a very successful 10-year-old party.

ELEVEN

Eleven-year-olds are not always at their best on home ground. But the social situation of a party, particularly if that party takes into account the nature and personality of the 11-year-old, allows them to appear at their vigorous, enthusiastic, boisterous best.

Eleven is not an age at which the two sexes get on well with each other socially, except under a controlled situation. It is usually best at this age to have all-girl or all-boy parties.

Eleven is not, like ten, a reasonably docile age at which the child easily and immediately obeys adult rules and commands. But if the rules are the rules of the game—that is quite a different matter. Thus, some athletic game with simple rules, which they themselves know and can apply, gives shape and structure to their play without arousing points of conflict between adult and child.

An outdoor setting, if available, provides opportunity for expression of the vigorous physical energies of the boy or girl at this age. The adult in charge will, of course, need to set a few outside limits, but she should accept the fact that not only physical but verbal energies tend to be somewhat out of bounds or rapidly shifting at this age, and demand opportunity for expression. A 12-year-old may throw food and may want to turn out all the lights or to play games involving physical contact with the opposite sex. ELEVEN is too hungry (and still too docile) to do much food throwing. And any drive he may feel toward interest in sex seems at this point easily satisfied by mildly lewd joking, which amuses the whole group immoderately and probably should not be too quickly or firmly squelched.

Interpersonal life at eleven can be extremely complex with a good deal of "not speaking" and excluding. Therefore a rather careful selection of guests may be necessary, particularly if these guests are girls. Better a small harmonious group than a larger group including some who at the moment may be bitter enemies.

Keep in mind, then, that 11-year-olds, especially boys, are as roly-poly, as high spirited, and as shapeless in their interrelations, physical and vocal, as a litter of puppies. Provide food and a place and opportunity for play and do not make too great or determined efforts to regulate or formalize their party behavior.

ELEVEN-YEAR-OLD PARTY

Key

Informality, separation of sexes, plenty of food, a small group of children who know each other well, and opportunity to play familiar games of which they thoroughly know the rules are the keys to success for a party at this age.

NUMBER OF GUESTS: Six to ten, all boys or all girls.

NUMBER OF ADULTS: One mother can do it alone, but one other adult can be a help if things get complicated. Also, a helper provides company for the mother.

Schedule

A supper party from 4 P.M. to 7 P.M. would be our suggestion.

4:00–4:10   Guests arrive, coming right from school. They usually arrive thirsty—so a drink should be provided at once. A good beverage is a combination of ginger ale and grape juice.

4:10–4:20 They all go out of doors for some vigorous physical activity—for instance, gathering firewood and building a stone or brick fireplace for cooking supper.

4:20–5:00 Some vigorous athletic game is good—some game which they play at school and with which they are, therefore, familiar. Dodge Ball is a good example. When tired or too hot children may flop on the ground, but they usually get right up again and maintain interest in such an activity for the better part of an hour.

Since they know the rules, virtually no adult direction or supervision is necessary. They can usually manage perfectly well by themselves. They not only are capable of but enjoy playing correctly, by rule.

5:00–5:45 Refreshments. Mother has prepared hamburger patties in advance. Hot dogs are also available, along with rolls, potato chips, and, for dessert, small cakes and ice cream. Many are not much interested in ice cream at this age, but cake is a great favorite. "Homemade" packaged frosted cakes are good. Large high cakes which cannot be held well in the hands are less successful. Likewise potato salad is usually less successful than the simpler potato chips. Milk and/or chocolate milk is a good beverage. Service for this meal is very casual. With a little help, the children can cook their own hot dogs or hamburgers. They sit or stand around an outdoor table. Usually all are sitting after the first few minutes.

This meal lasts quite a long time and the children enjoy not only the food but their own conversation. Adults if present are virtually ignored. Conversation tends to be extremely raucous and extremely uninhibited. Much giggling and joking—jokes being frankly crude and often vulgar: "For Chrysler's sake you son of a Buick, I'll kick you in the Nash" is the kind of saying they relish—and each one may take his turn at saying it. Then all roar with laughter.

Or they may discuss, with much humor, grammatical mistakes at school. Or discuss the teachers, repeating teachers' efforts at discipline: "None of your sass, Carlson," they may say, and then go off into gales of laughter. Or tell a joke about a teacher who reels into a PTA meeting drunk, demonstrating the way he reeled in.

65

Or they may do a great deal of clowning and burlesquing. A boy may have a trick arrow which gives the impression of going in one side of his head and coming out the other, or piercing his heart. Much dramatic "Oof!" "Ugh!" and pretending to kill themselves or to shoot each other.

5:45–6:00   Some more Dodge Ball or general violent horseplay.

6:00–7:00   Now they can come into the house and settle down to quiet play, with material provided by the host's mother. Having eaten, and with gross motor activity out of their systems, most are content to settle down to good, concentrated, quiet play. Making plastic models is a good activity for this period. These could be airplane models, boats, cars, in intricate and complex design. The mother furnishes materials needed, but usually no adult help is needed in construction. They are interested in the rules and most can follow them well.

These models may have been given out at the beginning of the party as favors, but the children don't play with them till the end of the party.

7:00   Host's mother (or father) takes home those who do not live within walking distance, or haven't come on their bikes.

Expenses

Total cost should not be more than $8 or at most $10. Main expense is the food. Models can be purchased for around 35¢ apiece.

Hints and Warnings

Remember that children of this age are extremely active. Considerable vigorous physical activity must be gotten out of the way before they are ready to settle down to fine motor activities.

This can be a very relaxed party. To a large extent the guests take over and enjoy themselves, by themselves. They will usually obey major adult suggestions, but the adult should not try to engineer things too much. They need considerable flexibility, plenty of space, plenty of physical activity, plenty of chance to be off by themselves, plenty of chance to talk. An outdoor party furnishes most of these opportunities—in fact, if the whole party were held indoors, things would probably not go very well.

Since interpersonal activity is so important here—especially the conversation—it is best to have children who know each other well. It is better not to invite strangers.

Adults should definitely not try to enter into the conversation, or to stimulate it in polite ways, such as asking, "What did you do at school?" Not only should adults not try to promote conversation; they should not try to squelch it even when it seems a trifle raucous. This is what children enjoy. Adults can be around, but children will—and prefer to— ignore them if allowed to do so.

Since there is much expressed hostility between the sexes at this age, it is most important to have the party for boys only, or for girls only. Don't try to mix the sexes. Also realize that younger siblings, especially of the opposite sex, if present may be a great nuisance.

If Party Is Given for Girls Instead of Boys

Girls don't need as violent activities as do boys, but they like much the same kind of outdoor physical activity, as, for instance, Dodge Ball. Girls' chatter tends to be more specific than boys'. They discuss their own thoughts and feelings, and especially like to talk about other children whom they're either mad about or hate like poison. They love to scramble around with each other on steamer rugs out on the ground, with lots of pillows to lie on, throw about, or snuggle up to. But it's better not to plan this kind of activity too definitely. A perceptive mother may suddenly realize that puppy-dog antics might be simulated by just such props as pillows and steamer rugs or old blankets. Throwing them down to the yard from an attic window (if you have an attic) adds that surprise note that ELEVEN so loves.

Twelve to Fifteen

The social whirl is on in these years from twelve to fifteen. Nothing starts a heart beating faster than the thought of a party—and no party is a party without both boys and girls. Baths are taken without a murmur, in preparation. In fact, parents of nonbathers might consider themselves lucky with their new silent partner, "Party," and put bathing in "Party's" hands, hoping there won't be too long an interval between.

With such high hopes and such a rush of enthusiasm and anticipation, it is sad to see how often the party-goer comes home crestfallen and bedraggled. He (or she) didn't really have a good time and he wonders what went wrong. This is far truer of girls than of boys, and more common at twelve and thirteen years of age than later.

Sadly enough, so much that went wrong could have been prevented by the parents if the party had only been more carefully planned and more closely supervised. The social structure of a party in the teens is complicated, and it takes a perceptive and quick-acting adult (or adults) to keep things going in the right direction.

Many parties are also unsuccessful because there is such a discrepancy between the social development of the boys and the girls at these ages. Someday, when the educator awakens to the knowledge that boys mature more slowly than girls and therefore should progress more slowly in school, parties won't produce as many failures as they do now. Twelve-year-old girls would be much happier with 13-year-old boys and vice versa. And 13-year-old girls would find a real 14-year-old shoulder to snuggle against while dancing, if such is the need, whereas a 13-year-old boy's shoulder is all too often uncomfortably low. Party crashing would be less of a problem if the boys were allowed to progress at their own rate, and were not pushed into immature behavior when social demands are too great.

Also, adults could be wiser in helping children to develop a social culture suitable to their age, within which they really can fit and enjoy themseves. Everything tends to be so speeded up in these United States that even party patterns are being affected. Ten- and 11-year-old girls are no longer allowed or helped to be their age, but often mimic 12- and 13-year-olds who in turn mimic adults. Why this has come to pass is hard to say. A similar situation is less common in Europe. Children are still children there. We might well learn from our European friends and bring back the vigor of the polka and the schottische so much more suitable to the enthusiasm and strong rhythmic needs of the 12-year-old than ballroom dancing. Or our own Virginia reel or square dance with the control and fun of the caller could also be very successful at twelve years.

By fourteen the choice of activity is more readily in the party-goer's hands. By this age he not only dances with ease but also has enough social poise to make dancing enjoyable. Even so, he is more apt to choose the more casual and informal, the sudden spontaneous party of close friends, with more time given to listening to records and talking than to dancing.

By fifteen more elaborate planning is in order, not just on the part of the party-giver, but often also on the part of the group which will attend. Parties may be most successful when they become a joint affair in their planning and preparation. Guests can be really a part of the party from beginning to end.

Perhaps it is in part this intimate participation which can make parties at this age so successful, in contrast to those more awkward beginning parties at twelve and thirteen, when expectations are so high and endings may all too often prove disappointing.

TWELVE

Twelve is a particularly difficult age to have a party, not only because of the tendency to wildness on the part of the boys, but because of their inclination to hold back and not participate in planned activities. It is difficult also because twelve is such an in-between age so far as both boys and girls are concerned. At this age many are neither children nor adults. Some are extremely sophisticated (in their own estimation, at least); others are extremely immature. And the same individual may vary as an evening progresses.

Children are sophisticated enough to recognize good food, but immature enough to gobble it all up or to throw it. They are sophisticated enough to criticize "babyish" activities, but not sophisticated enough to take part smoothly in dancing activities without considerable encouragement. They may be sophisticated enough to criticize the behavior of adults in charge, yet immature enough still to need constant supervision. They are sophisticated enough to be somewhat drawn to the opposite sex, but not enough to know always just how to behave with the opposite sex.

Twelve-year-olds also are usually very self-conscious and reluctant to attempt anything new. They prefer activities which they already know and are good at. Any host or hostess who tries to introduce new games too quickly will get little or no cooperation.

There is likely, at twelve, to be a great discrepancy between the interests of boys and of girls. Girls are usually more mature, more interested in personal-social relationships, and much more interested in the opposite sex than are boys. Boys are more immature, and are more interested in other boys (they will ask what other *boys* are going to be at the party), and in clowning. Girls may have crushes on certain boys and pin high hopes on getting some attention from these boys at the party. Boys may not be at all interested in girls, and may find their interest "bothersome and sickening."

The attitude of TWELVES toward adult supervision, like other aspects of their behavior, is extremely variable. Some are respectful and reasonably docile. Others will be resistant and wisecracking. Adults at a party are, in the opinion of many 12-year-olds, there *to work*, and not to enjoy themselves.

There is likely to be considerable interest in tactile contact between boys and girls at this age. The girls have a real romantic interest in this. In boys it is more exploratory, or being silly, or in the nature of roughhousing. But both gravitate toward it, whatever their motives may be. Adults should expect this kind of interest and allow it to be exploited in a legitimate and somewhat controlled way, as for instance in a flashlight dance or in the Marshmallow Game.

A party at this age can quickly and irretrievably go out-of-bounds. It is possible to keep wildness at a minimum by limiting the space used so that it can all be supervised. Planning should be detailed though flexible. But keep in mind that a party at this age can end in pandemonium and disaster. This is especially true in relation to food. Even the best-behaved TWELVES do seem stimulated to bad behavior by the presence of food. They throw food, squirt drinks, make spitballs of their paper napkins, toss food in the air and catch it in their mouths, mix and mess up food and drink. Boys are the worst offenders, but if somebody throws food at a girl, she is likely to throw it back.

It is for these reasons that an outdoor beach party or picnic is often preferred by parents. Outdoor activities can sometimes absorb tensions which seem to rise indoors. Thus it might be better to postpone a party until the weather is favorable than to harbor the memory of a disastrous indoor party.

INDOOR PARTY AT TWELVE

Key

Though the child giving this party should definitely be consulted, and all plans made with him in advance, nevertheless the adult must be constantly present while the party is taking place, to hold it well in control, as a party at this age can easily go to pieces. It is essential, also, that the adult in charge have a clear understanding of the 12-year-old personality, so that he will know exactly what to provide, and what to avoid. Though TWELVES love parties, their parties can become extremely chaotic unless kept well in hand by the adults who are supervising.

Many TWELVES like dancing and will dance once they are warmed up. However, for most 12-year-old boys, dancing is not enough. For them, games, competitions, prize-giving must supplement the dancing. And food, of course, must be provided in large quantities.

NUMBER OF GUESTS: Twelve is a good number, if possible girls and boys evenly matched.

NUMBER OF ADULTS: Three, or better four, strong, active, quick-witted adults. Usually host or hostess's parents and one other couple.

Schedule

Good hours are 8 to 10 P.M.

8:00–8:15   Some initial warming-up activity. The choice will depend on the group. With a spontaneous, alive group, an enjoyable game can be stimulated by pinning the name of a famous person on the back of each guest as he enters. With this clue, the others treat each one as befits the person he is supposed to represent, until finally he guesses who he is. Great hilarity often ensues.

           Other groups need more prepared planning which demands less of them. You can show a cartoon movie for such groups, or have a magician or a puppet show. The cartoon movie (though some might think it young for twelve) is probably the best. (You can rent these, as well as a projector if you don't have one or can't borrow one, from an optical store.) Not only do TWELVES enjoy a cartoon, but since there is little plot, those who come late aren't missing anything.

8:15–8:20   If this is a birthday party, presents can be opened right at this point.

8:20–8:40   The next activity should be arranged with a view to what the group has been accustomed to doing together. If, for instance, they all (or mostly) go to the same dancing class, they might start right in dancing at this point. Otherwise, or if they need more warming up, it is a good idea to have

75

some "intellectual" activity, such as Charades, or Twenty Questions. This can go on for twenty minutes or so, but should be terminated quickly when interest starts to falter.

8:40–10:00   Dancing (on the terrace or piazza if weather allows). Interspersed with games.

Dancing is the activity most generally enjoyed by TWELVES. However, girls may be more enthusiastic about this than boys. To capture and hold the interest of boys, some competitive games should be interspersed. And even the dances may best be given a competitive turn.

Refreshments are extremely important at this age. You will need to provide *quantities* of punch and cookies. Cookies should be homemade and *good*. You can serve soft drinks instead of punch if you prefer, but punch is cheaper. However, the quality of the punch is very important. Potato chips are good to serve, but peanuts stimulate throwing.

Have all this food out on a long table, buffet style, near the dancers, for them to take as they wish. Put it out when the dancing starts. Have this refreshment table in a corner of the dancing room and be sure that an adult is nearby to supervise the food.

The games should match girls against boys. A good one is Marshmallow on a String. (A marshmallow is threaded in the middle of a two-foot-long string. A row of girls faces a row of boys, each boy-girl couple having a marshmallow on a string between them. Each chews the string, trying to reach the marshmallow first. Prizes are given for individuals or for teams.)

Another good game is to have the girls all line up behind a sheet which has holes cut in it to allow their noses to stick through. The boys attempt to guess which nose belongs to which girl, writing down their guesses. A prize is given to the one having the most correct guesses.

To get things started, a Card-Matching Dance makes a good take-off. Playing cards can be torn in two, then partners are determined by whoever holds the matching half of the card.

To keep things going, two good dances are a Balloon Dance and a Personality Dance. In the Balloon Dance, couples dance with a balloon pressed between their foreheads and hands behind their backs. The couple which manages to continue the longest without dropping or breaking the balloon wins. . . . In the Personality Dance, couples are eliminated one by one, according to any arbitrary rule which the "caller" determines. Thus everyone wearing a wrist watch might have to sit down. Then everyone who has not been to Washington, etc. The couple remaining on the floor longest gets a prize.

10:00   Party terminates. It works out best if the host or hostess's parents, and the helping couple, drive guests home. This is the best way to get them out of the house. Otherwise they may be just warming up and not want to go home. Or, if your scheduled plans have been run through, they may be getting wild.

Expenses

This need not be an expensive party to give. Cookies and punch, if you make the cookies yourself, should not come to more than $6. Prizes will be around $6. Film should be available for $1 or so. Thus the party need not cost more than $15, unless renting of projector brings it over that.

Hints and Warnings

It is ideal to have the sexes evenly matched. But you may need to invite a few extra boys, as some may back out at the last minute. Or they may turn out to be duds as far as participating in the dancing is concerned.

During the initial showing of the cartoons, or whatever activity takes place first, an alert parent can spot twosomes who are going to be troublemakers. (You can tell because they will poke, hit, or punch each other, giggle a good deal, wrestle with each other.) Then by adroit planning you may be able to keep them somewhat separated. (Parents may think that cartoon movies are too young for TWELVES, but most, unless very sophisticated, do like them.)

Use Charades or other warming-up games if necessary. But if the guests are used to dancing with each other they may like this best and may want to start right in with this, right after the movies, without wasting any time in warming up.

77

Note the importance of interspersing the dancing with competitive games. And of keeping dancing interesting to the boys by not having it be just plain dancing. Some boys absolutely will not dance unless it is a prize dance.

You will find that four adults (parents and two other helpers) are not too many. There is a *good deal* for an adult to do: running phonograph and supervising choice of records; supervising the refreshment table *constantly*, not only to prevent the misuse of food, but to keep replenishing the constantly disappearing supply of food and drink; washing out cups and glasses if paper cups run out; giving out prizes; keeping the dances going.

Prizes: small stuffed animals or cosmetics for the girls. Or candy bars, nickels and dimes (money is very acceptable at this age), magic equipment, passes to the movies or to a miniature golf course, bolo bats.

With less mature or less socially sophisticated children, you will find that you may need to spend more time with games and less with dancing. Or, in addition to keeping the dancing lively and interesting for the boys by having prize dances, in some communities children may prefer such kinds of dancing as square dancing or a Virginia reel.

Refreshments: Both punch and cookies must be *really* good, or guests will make adverse and extremely biting comments, which by next day will be spread all over town. A good punch is made of ginger ale (a good grade of ginger ale) mixed with pineapple or grapefruit juice.

It is very important to have the refreshments in the same room as the dancing. Otherwise you will need an extra adult to supervise the refreshment room. Also boys might then hang around in the extra room and not dance, and it gives guests a chance to disperse and wander around the house. If they do this, they will take advantage of their freedom and may do such things as calling up their teachers and kidding with them, or calling strange numbers picked at random from the phone book.

OUTDOOR PARTY AT TWELVE

Key

An outdoor party at this age has both advantages and disadvantages. It is harder to control, and the children may become wilder. On the other hand, there is certainly less breakage, and out-of-bounds behavior

The separation of the sexes

Above left: Three-legged race

Above right: Inner-tube race

Right: Sack race

Cooling

Prizes for the winners

Top left: Marshmallow on a string

Top right: Balloon dance

cal chairs

Pass the orange

Top left: Guessing noses

Top right: Horseplay

Twelve-year-old dancing

Happy ending

out of doors is apt not to be so worrisome to the adult. Most Twelves thoroughly enjoy an out-of-doors party.

Necessary ingredients, to insure success, are constant planned activity (especially activities which match one sex against the other), plenty of food, prizes for everything, and a good deal of firm supervision to keep things from getting entirely out of hand.

Number of Guests: Twelve to twenty boys and girls. An outdoor party can handle more guests than an indoor party.

Number of Adults: Preferably two couples. The host's mother and father and one other couple. Mothers alone should not attempt to control Twelves, especially not frail, frightened mothers.

Schedule

A supper (or luncheon) picnic at a beach, public park, or even in a large back yard is a good choice at this age. If a supper picnic, the hours might be 4:00 to 6:30. Assuming that the party is a beach party, and that it is being held in the spring or fall (in the summer the party might be just a swimming and eating party, but often children are away and planned parties for Twelves are not given then), the schedule might be as follows:

4:00–4:05 Guests all gather at the host's home. Boys and girls will at first be entirely separated at this age, no mingling. It is up to the adult to see that the sexes mix. This can be done, to begin with, by having them draw straws to see which car they go in. This tends to mix boys and girls slightly.

4:05–4:15 Drive to beach (if it is nearby. Otherwise you will of course have to allow more time). As they drive along, they can play various car games such as looking for out-of-state license plates. A score is kept by an adult in the car. Persons with the highest scores receive prizes on reaching their destination.

4:15–4:25 Arrive at beach. The boundaries should at once be explained to all guests. These will have been staked off in advance, with ropes, otherwise guests are apt to stray all over the beach and out of sight.

4:25–5:05 Games such as Kick Ball, Volley Ball, or Baseball. All play. Games should be familiar ones which all know and like.

83

Have two teams, the captain of each being chosen by the adults. Then each captain chooses a boy, girl, boy, girl, etc., till all are chosen. A game like this helps guests to loosen up, and to expend energy. It also helps the boys and girls to mingle, though not intimately enough to embarrass them.

5:05–5:35   Relay races, with mixed boy-girl teams, adults supervising closely. Prizes are given to the winners. Various kinds of relay races are good, among them:

> Three-Legged Race—a boy and a girl, with one leg of each tied together.
>
> Sack Race—tied into a sack together, a boy and girl hop along.
>
> Inner-Tube Race—boy and girl in blown-up inner tube race with another pair similarly encumbered.
>
> Paper-Bag Race—each contestant races alone to the end of a line, gets a paper bag, blows it up, pops it, and races back.

They may want to repeat some of the more popular of these, and should be allowed to do so if time permits.

5:35–6:20   Refreshments. Ordinary picnic rations—hot dogs, potato chips, toasted marshmallows. Adults need to have the wood and charcoal for the fire ready in advance. Boys and girls cook their own hot dogs and marshmallows. A big ice bucket with soft drinks and bottle openers should be available throughout, since guests become very thirsty and may need repeated drinks as they play games, as well as during the meal.

6:20–6:30   Guests taken home.

Expenses

Food and drink for this party may be fairly expensive, as children have big appetites at this age. Food for a party of twenty might cost around $12. Prizes would probably amount to at least another $5. Thus the expense could run up to around $20, but this would depend on how many guests you have, and on how expensive the prizes are.

Hints and Warnings

Most of the hints and warnings which apply to an indoor party at this age also apply out of doors. However, supervision of an outdoor party is in some ways even more difficult, since the outdoor setting allows the more adventuresome guests to wander off. Also, outdoors may bring out even worse fooling, jumping around, wrestling, silly behavior, misuse of food, throwing things in general, than does indoors. In fact, out-of-bounds behavior is pretty constant, especially during any transitions. Therefore, not only is it essential to have a father present, but the adult guest couple should be a really effective and helpful couple who understand and can cope with children of this age.

The big advantage of a party of this kind is that 12-year-olds enjoy it so much. The outdoor setting allows them to feel relaxed and free. Especially do they enjoy the outdoor meal. Spontaneous singing is apt to spring up during the party and also during the ride home.

It is very important to define clearly the beach boundaries when the party first starts. Otherwise, even with the aid of a whistle (which is essential), it may be hard to keep the group rounded up.

Prizes: Remember that each time a prize is given, a whole team will have to be rewarded, so the number of prizes can mount up rapidly. It saves confusion for an adult to keep score as to which team wins each event, then the final score can be computed. Prizes should be kept in baskets, one basket each for boys and girls. Wrapping the presents and allowing guests to grab for them prevents the first choosers from selecting all the "best" prizes. Prizes, as with the indoor party, can include small stuffed animals, any cosmetics, pocketbooks for girls, pencils, candy bars, nickels and dimes, any kind of free pass, bolo bats.

Boy-girl interrelations, though awkward, are an important part of a party at this age. The sexes do not mix at all well. In fact, if they are going to get together very much, the adult has to get them together and keep them together. They like being together but are too self-conscious in most instances to do much about it. However, boys and girls are very much aware of each other, and the notion of kissing games is apt to come up spontaneously. Adults should be prepared for this in advance, and know what they are going to do about it. A fairly tight schedule can help to discourage this kind of activity if you don't want to permit it.

THIRTEEN

One outstanding characteristic of the typical 13-year-old must be kept strongly in mind if any party at this age is to be a success. It is that the boy or girl at this age feels a strong need to withdraw from any adult supervision, and from what he considers adult prying. It is perhaps the need to withdraw from supervision and observation, quite as much as any real need or desire to be alone with a member of the opposite sex, which drives THIRTEENS at a party to turn out all the lights, or if outdoors, to seek the darkest shadows of the lawn.

Recognizing this strong drive, adults in charge of a 13-year-old party will firmly and efficiently give what help is needed (especially in relation to providing music and food), but will for the most part remain discreetly on the edge of things. That is, they should give the help necessary (and this will still be quite a good deal), but should depend to quite an extent on the judgment of host or hostess as to whether this particular party needs more games or more dancing. A boy or girl of thirteen plays very different roles in relation to his mother and father, and to his friends; and parents should de-emphasize the parent-child relationship during a party.

FOURTEEN does a pretty good job of ignoring adults at a party. THIRTEEN, uncertain and in some conflict with himself, will engage in conflict with his parents at a party unless parents arm themselves against this contingency by careful advance planning and by the exercise of much objectivity and humor, or perhaps by providing a good substitute whom their son or daughter will respect.

THIRTEEN's drives toward socializing with members of the opposite sex are as a rule at rather a beginning stage. A girl may try to snuggle on a boy's shoulder as she dances (made somewhat difficult by the fact that she may be towering above him), but both boys and girls still feel quite free to complain about each other's poor dancing. The girls falter between coquetry and sociability. Boys slip quickly back to roughhousing if things are not going smoothly.

With FOURTEENS, a party can continue successfully even though several slips of timing or action have been made. At thirteen, the balance between success and failure is extremely delicate. It is easy for a party to fail at thirteen, through an unwise choice of guests, because you fail to get them warmed up and started, or because the party is pitched at a too mature or too immature level for the invited guests.

THIRTEEN-YEAR-OLD DANCING PARTY

Key

Probably the most important thing here is to choose guests who are all of approximately the same level of social maturity. If all the boys are old enough to be interested in dancing (which may mean that some of them need to be fourteen), everyone will have a better time. There will be less roughhousing and less need for the games which the more mature children dislike.

Parents should remain on the margin of things, though a firm father in charge of the phonograph is essential.

87

Thirteen-Year-Old Dancing Party

Some degree of semi-darkness is much desired and some, though not excessive, fooling with lights might be permitted.

An outdoor setting, if the season permits, helps a great deal in the first few stiff minutes. A slow start is to be expected and the party moves into better form if the group is allowed to find itself, even if they do this in rather a slow, bumbling way. Once dancing has started, except for an interval for food, most will be content simply to be left alone to continue dancing.

NUMBER OF GUESTS: Depends chiefly on size of house or dancing area. Six to a dozen couples might be a good number.

NUMBER OF ADULTS: Parents of host or hostess, and one other couple for moral support of the parents.

Schedule

The party should start around 8 o'clock and will be terminated by parents calling for guests around 10:30.

8:00–8:15   Guests arrive, brought individually or in groups by parents. During this preliminary period, boys and girls mill around in entirely separate groups. There is almost no crossing of sex lines. This initial stiff period of non-mingling is much less stiff and embarrassing if guests can be out of doors. Initial forays, by girls, toward the boys' group may come to little.

8:15   Finally, (with luck), after not more than fifteen minutes, and with some encouragement from the adults (Father may announce over a loud-speaker, if an outdoor party, that it is now time to choose partners), dancing may start. Usually one of the more forward girls, or some girl who has a more or less steady boy friend, will start it by saying to her companion, "Come on. let's dance."
            If they absolutely cannot get themselves started, a Cinderella Dance, in which each girl throws one shoe into the middle of the floor and the boys each choose a shoe and then find a partner whose other shoe matches, will get things going.

8:15–9:30   Once dancing starts, it should catch on well and nearly all participate in every dance. At first boys may be fairly polite

88

about choosing different partners, but shortly certain couples (boys and girls who know and like each other well) may pretty much stick together.

Dances are short, so there is opportunity for frequent changing. Boys and girls may complain about each others' dancing.* There is considerable self-consciousness. If a couple should discover themselves alone on the floor they will usually leave and wait till dancing is more general. Boys usually thank partners at end of each dance.

The father who is directing affairs may call out, "Girls' choice," to vary things occasionally.

If younger or less mature boys have been invited, they may, as the evening progresses, cease to dance and start chasing each other around, which will leave some of the girls out of things. Some girls may dance with each other.

9:30–9:45 Refreshments. The time of refreshments should be flexible. If interest in dancing wanes sooner than expected, refreshments can be brought in earlier.

Refreshments, consisting of soft drinks, sandwiches, and cake may be served on a long table. Guests get food and wander about as they eat. They do not necessarily sit down. Allow four bottles of soft drink per child, as they will continue drinking during the rest of the evening.

9:45–9:55 Transitions are difficult at this age. To get guests back to dancing, if they have wandered about, a Spot Dance is useful. Lights off, couples dance, mother from a vantage point (as upstairs window if party is out of doors) shines a flashlight beam on one couple at a time. The last couple on the floor wins a prize—one prize for the girl, one for the boy.

9:55–10:30 Dancing continues. Earlier in the evening guests will have wanted fast music. Now as a more romantic atmosphere pervades, chances are that they may want slower music.

---

* Degree of dancing skill varies considerably. Some of the more mature girls may try to snuggle, but this is in some cases difficult since they may be larger than their partners. Some converse smoothly; others look stiff and self-conscious and concerned about their dancing. Boy may complain to other boy, "These girls can't dance." Other boy replies, "You've got to put *life* into them."

10:30   Parents call for them to transport them home. Plans have been made in advance as to who will transport whom, so that not every parent has to be involved.

Expenses

This does not need to be an expensive party. Since prizes are few, their cost can be minimal. Presumably the host owns or can borrow a record player and what records are needed. Thus the main cost is for soft drinks, for sandwiches, and for cake.

Hints and Warnings

The most successful party at this age will be one where guests are carefully chosen and are all more or less at the same level of maturity. That is, preferably choose boys who are old enough to be willing to dance. Or have all young enough to be willing to take part in prize dances and competitive games, more as in a 12-year-old party.

A 13-year-old party is often planned for the whole class, particularly in small private schools. However, at this age perhaps more than at any other, we find tremendously different levels of social maturity. Within any one class there will be many different groups, each with a different notion of what is fun to do at a party. The girls, however, are fairly pliable, regardless of their maturity level. The boys are less flexible. Some boys want to dance and only to dance, like girls, and *can't stand* games and prizes. Others want games, don't want to dance, and really prefer to roughhouse and to throw food. So that if the type of party being given doesn't fit their interests, boys tend to behave badly. (At twelve, different levels of maturity and of interest don't seem to do too much harm. Even the more mature boys are content to sink back to "hacking around," and the girls don't mind too much how the boys behave, and don't expect too much of them.)

It is very important to have an even number of girls and of boys, or perhaps even more boys than girls. Any girls left over and not danced with feel, and are, extremely conspicuous at this age.

It is also important to have a good firm father (and one with a good sense of humor) running the phonograph. The music must be kept going. The difficulty here is that likes and dislikes are *very* strong, and not particularly unified. The group *can't stand* certain records— "*Nobody* can dance to that." They groan and shout complaints about ones they don't like. Whatever record is played (with one or two exceptions) arouses objections from somebody. Father should try, within reason, to adapt to the demands of the group, but only within reason.

Keeping the dances short helps, particularly early in the evening when some of the boys may be dancing with certain girls to be polite and not because they like the girls or even can dance well together.

The whole problem of lighting is quite central and vital at this age. Boys and girls of thirteen do not like too much light. In an outdoor party, for instance, when the dancing is on the terrace, if too bright lights are turned on, guests seem automatically driven to the shadows of the lawn, even though dancing on the grass is not too practical. It is probably best to have rather dim lights, and even to turn these out on occasion—as for instance in the Spot Dance. Probably some fooling with lights is inevitable, even on the part of the more mature boys. It seems essential to boys and girls of this age to get lights off, even though most do not, within the confines of a party, make much of the opportunity once the lights are off. Too much light attracts adverse remarks from guests: "Oh no!" "It attracts the bugs" "Turn those lights off" "I don't care *how soon* this party ends with all those lights on!" Mothers often complain that all the children want at these parties is *the dark*. Possibly parents worry too much about this.

As to refreshments—be sure that there is plenty to drink. The quantity of sandwiches and cake is not so important as the quantity of liquid refreshment. Also, it is important to have the food *all ready* before guests are summoned to eat.

An easily available bathroom is quite important. There is considerable nervousness at a party at this age, and it is often expressed in a need to go to the bathroom. Since this is rather embarrassing to many, bathroom facilities should be easily available, and directions for reaching them clear and evident.

The presence of at least one set of parents is essential, but parents should remain on the sidelines and not be too conspicuously present. Father is quite necessary to run the phonograph; mother to provide food and any prizes and to run the Spot Dance. Parents, however, should try not to interfere too much and should not try to run the party *their way*. Otherwise considerable conflict between host or hostess and parents may develop right on the spot, as both sides take out their anxieties that it may not be a good party on each other.

We should like to emphasize once more that if guests are all fully into thirteen and equally mature, for the most part plain dancing, without prizes or devices for getting them started, and without competitive games, will probably be most satisfactory. If guests tend to be rather immature or somewhat unsophisticated, a 12-year-old-type party with prize dances and games will be best. If the group is mixed, the more mature will scorn games, the less mature will not be satisfied with dancing.

If the choice of guests has not been ideal in this respect, and you find that some want to do one kind of thing and some another, great flexibility on the part of the host and of his parents will be needed. You will have to try one kind of thing but be quick to shift and substitute another if necessary. Probably in such instances, the host's judgment of what the other children want may be better than the parents'.

In our experience, enjoying parties which feature competitive games and prize dances seems to be a stage which most boys and girls do savor for a season and then outgrow. Thus if the children in your community have had a season of this kind of party when they were twelve, they will probably have outgrown them by thirteen. But if such parties are arranged for them for the first time when they are thirteen, they may be more tolerant of this type of activity.

FOURTEEN

Fourteen is an enthusiastic age. The boy or girl of this age exhibits great enthusiasm, remarkable energy, and a tremendous appetite for any adventure—particularly for adventure involving the opposite sex.

Thus, he or she is inevitably party-minded. A dinner or dancing party, or even a plain Coke party, if well run, provides welcome opportunities for boy-girl encounters. An all-night pajama party for girls, as well as the endless telephoning which goes on at this age, can be the occasion for discussions about boys which are almost as important and satisfactory as the boys themselves.

FOURTEEN is expansive as well as energetic and enthusiastic. Many FOURTEENS would give a party every week if permitted, and would invite everybody in the class. Reasonable parental restraint must be laid down.

Fourteen-year-old girls are often more than a bit silly and extreme in their enthusiasm about boys. Fortunately, most tend to be a bit restrained at any boy-girl party, and show themselves at their giggliest only at all-girl affairs.

Fourteen is not an age when appreciation of parents is conspicuous. Thus it is not to be expected that parents will play a major social role at a 14-year-old party. They will need to provide food and discreet chaperoning, but very much from the sidelines.

Fortunately, most 14-year-olds are reasonably decorous at a party —at least they do not wrestle or throw food, or drink too much— so that chaperoning does not include disciplining. Transportation often seems to be a parent's major function in the social life of FOURTEEN, and in suburban communities somebody often has to give up quite a lot of time and energy to this cause.

Most FOURTEENS not only love the idea of parties but enjoy the parties themselves tremendously (aside from the occasional shyness of a boy or girl who is not fully one of the crowd or fully at home with the opposite sex, or the occasional tragedy of a broken heart, which may become broken right in the midst of a social evening). Thus, most party-givers consider the all-round pleasure resulting from a party quite worth any effort and expense involved in giving it.

Fourteen is an expansive age and we find ourselves expanding here in our party suggestions. A variety of parties is suggested because of the fact that, in many ways, fourteen is an ideal party age.

FOURTEEN-YEAR-OLD DINNER PARTY

Key

The key here is a great deal of detailed planning and considerable hard work before the party, as well as very hard work during the party, so that the handling of the large number of guests goes on as expeditiously as possible. Adults need to regard themselves as caterers, cooks, janitors, doormen—this is not a party for the adult to enjoy while it is going on. But when it is over, if it has been successful, adults will be left with a tremendous feeling of accomplishment in that a group of stiff and rather awkward teen-agers will have been put on a relaxed, friendly footing ready to enjoy the dance which is to follow.

Though we introduce a dinner party preceding a dance here at fourteen, there is perhaps more age difference with regard to this kind of party from one community to another than in respect to almost any other type of party. We have known of 12-year-olds for whom dinner parties preceding dances were arranged. On the other hand, this kind of entertainment does not come in some communities till boys and girls are fifteen or sixteen; and in fact in some places may never occur. However, a dinner party preceding a dance can set the mood of the dance and often, with the ice already broken beforehand, can insure the success of the dance.

NUMBER OF GUESTS: Anywhere from twelve to fifty, depending on the size of the house and on how many parents are available to share the large amount of work and rather large expenses.

NUMBER OF PARENTS: At least two sets of parents. If there is a large number of guests, more parents are needed. Also one or two helpers to keep the dishes washed.

Schedule

Before the party: The main purpose of this party is to feed the guests, to get them warmed up and relaxed for the dance which is to follow, and to get them paired off. Hostess (hostesses) makes a list and decides on the pairings, though of course respecting any preferences. Otherwise, couples tend to go by size. Both names are printed on folded blank visiting cards and given out before supper. The couples then get together. The party should start about 7:30 for a dance at 9.

7:15–7:45   Guests arrive, brought singly or in groups by their parents. They gather in the yard (if weather permits), for the most part boys together and girls together. A little mingling, but very little. Most are rather stiff. Some drink punch which is available in a large bowl on a table—ginger ale and frozen lemon juice.

Phonograph is going throughout. Records are brought by the girls. Some one individual, for instance a younger brother of the hostess, keeps the music going.

Some of the older boys may gather in quite a sophisticated manner by the punch bowl. There will be some mingling of sexes as time wears on, but usually very little.

7:45–8:00   Now that all have arrived, the hostess hands out cards with names of couples, and couples locate each other.

8:00–8:20 Refreshments are announced. Food is available, buffet style, on a long table in the living room. Platters of roast beef, turkey, potato salad, green salad, hot buttered rolls if desired. China plates, knives and forks, napkins, paper cups. Beverage is more punch, or water.

Guests come in and fill plates, then take them out into the garden or into the living room. Though the meal is served buffet style, they seem to prefer to sit in chairs and, if possible, around tables—which should be available at intervals. Guests sit at this meal in the couples to which they have been assigned. Though some couples are relaxed, some are rather stiff at first.

Through this meal, guests usually behave quite sedately. There may be a very little clowning toward the end of the meal. Hostesses are busy keeping an eye on things throughout. Parents are very busy seeing that everyone is fed. Helpers are also busy in the kitchen.

Behavior from couple to couple, and from table to table, may vary greatly. Some flirt and laugh; at some tables conversation is general; at some one boy may hold forth; at others things may be stiffer.

8:20–8:35 Dessert is now served to them, after empty plates have been taken to the kitchen. Dessert may be strawberries on vanilla ice cream. As they finish eating (adults collect the plates), boys and girls tend to re-group in the earlier separate-sex groups, though a few of the more mature couples may stay together. Some remain at the tables; some wander about the yard. There is a little throwing of wadded-up napkins by boys, and a little squealing by the girls: "Hurt more than my pride. Hurt my face." "You're going to get this water pitcher right over your head."

8:45 Girls all come in to primp. Boys stay, momentarily, downstairs or in the yard.

8:48 Boys come in, streaming through the house and making for the bus hired to drive them to the dance.

8:50 Now girls come downstairs and out into the bus. A few couples sit together, but most of the boys have grouped together on entering the bus.

8:52   The bus drives off.

9:00–12:00 or 1:00   Dance. Afterward transported home by parents, car pools having been arranged beforehand.

Expenses

Expenses vary directly with the number of guests. This is not an inexpensive party to give, but the cost to any one family can be cut down by having several girls give the party together.

For fifty guests, with the menu described above, with $10 for the bus and $5 for two helpers to wash the dishes, the cost is about $75, which if shared by three amounts to $25 apiece.

Hints and Warnings

This party can be given for almost any number of guests. Obviously, the larger the party, the greater the work and the expense, but both can be cut down by having several girls get together as hostesses.

FOURTEEN is so expansive that he just naturally likes to invite everybody in the class. Also, this may be the custom in some communities. However, by inviting say twelve or even fewer couples, the whole thing can be simplified tremendously. This would cut down on expense, number of dishes, amount of food, and amount of space needed. In case of rain, unless you had a very large house, more than twenty-five guests would be a problem.

Fourteen-year-olds behave much better at a party than do 12- and 13-year-olds. Though there tends to be a great variation in degree of sophistication, even the least sophisticated do not, as at a 13-year-old party, revert to physical wildness, turning off lights, throwing food. Also at fourteen there is no longer conflict between parent and child. Now parents and hosts are allies, trying to make the party go smoothly.

Experience shows that you can't always tell just where the group will gather (assuming that space permits any choice). That is, you don't know in which part of the garden they will group, or whether they will prefer indoors or outdoors. Thus as far as possible you need to be prepared to shift from original plans.

Guest list may include all the girls in the class. Then an equal number of boys is invited. If the dance which follows is especially exclusive, only boys and girls are invited who are on the dance list.

If guests are fed immediately on arrival, there tends to be a disorganized, restless period after the meal and before it is time to leave for the dance. It is best to have the informal period first. Then they eat and then it is time to leave, right away, for the dance.

Music throughout, with someone arranged for in advance to keep the phonograph going, helps a good deal and adds a good deal. But guests should *not* be urged to dance. As a rule they do not want to dance so early in the evening.

Adults must be prepared to work hard, not only at the party but during the day. If a large number of guests is invited, it may take two mothers and two girls much of a day to get food ready, dishes all ready, flowers ready, everything prepared. While the guests are actually present, the work is constant and intense.

Adults should not expect to have much attention paid to them. One father of a 14-year-old, attending her party, commented afterward that he had never been greeted by so many "glazed expressions" in his life. Guests will probably say "Thank you" as they leave, little more.

If you serve cold meat, you may be able to get the butcher to slice it for you after it has been cooked. This will save a good deal of trouble. It is important to try to be original about the food and not to serve exactly what all the other mothers have served. In some communities, chicken à la king on rice has become a joke. Try to be a little different.

Since most, especially the girls, do not eat their rolls, and since these are the only last-minute thing which has to be served hot, the meal and service can be simplified greatly by omitting the rolls.

Because all want food at once, it takes several adults to get the food onto the plates quickly. However, appetites vary tremendously. Girls, for instance, are usually not hungry. Thus, if an adult does serve, there is a great deal of waste. Therefore it might be best if guests could be channeled into the dining room a little more slowly, by having a father stand at the door for instance, and then they could serve themselves and might take only as much as they wanted.

A good supply of folding chairs might help, as at this age nobody seems to want to sit on the floor, ground, or edge of the terrace (at least at this kind of party).

Transportation to the dance can be simplified tremendously by hiring a bus. A bus to accommodate forty or more can probably be hired for around $10.

FOURTEEN-YEAR-OLD PAJAMA PARTY

Key

Informality; plenty of food; a choice of guests who know each other intimately and who like each other; staying overnight; and not too much adult supervision and interference are the important things here. It works out best if the guests can have a separate wing of a house or at least a separate room or rooms and bath, or even a separate beach cottage with parents nearby. An adult, or adults, in close contact, not only will tend to become very much annoyed, but also will put a damper on the party.

NUMBER OF GUESTS: Six girls.

NUMBER OF ADULTS: None right on the spot. Parents will be, and should be, in the background. A sympathetic adult guest, or couple, might help.

Schedule

Party can start around 5 P.M. and will probably last till around 11 A.M. the next morning.

5:00–6:00   Girls arrive, are greeted by the hostess and immediately want to get off by themselves to talk and giggle. Then they listen to records or to the radio, or just talk.

6:00–7:00   Dinner. Guests tend suddenly to become very hungry. A full meal is served to them, which might consist of fried chicken, potato chips, salad, cheese, French bread, soft drinks. They usually eat every bit of food available, even though there may be much conversation about dieting.

7:00–9:00   Girls go to the movies or at least for a walk. It is really too early to get into their pajamas; and if they stay at home at this point, word is apt to get around and boys collect from nowhere. Girls don't mind this, but parents may wish to avoid it.

9:00–9:30   They come home, put on shortie pajamas, set each other's hair or even cut each other's hair—anyway much fussing with hair. Then they plan future parties.

Food is provided at this point. They will need a good deal, to last them through the night. For a party of six, we would suggest the following evening and night refreshments:

4 packages of cream-filled cookies
2 homemade frosted cakes—chocolate and white
2 large packages of potato chips
Bottled soft drinks—at least 2 or 3 apiece

9:30–10:00 Pre-bedtime card game, a formal finishing of the evening and signal for bedtime—at least for the theoretical bedtime.

10:00–4:00 Theoretically, bedtime at 10 P.M. However, now comes perhaps the "best" part of the party. Girls are up and down and many do not actually go to sleep till as late as 4 A.M. They talk, play tricks, eat. Among the tricks are "short-sheeting the beds." If a girl gets up to go to the bathroom, others fold up her sheet so that she can't stretch her legs down. . . . Girls lock other girls in the bathroom. . . . Take all the covers off a girl's bed and hide them . . . Put things, as a banana peel, in girl's bed . . . *Much* talk about boys. Much giggling.

4:00–10:00 A.M. Sleep. (Some of course will have gone to sleep earlier.)

10:00–11:00 A.M. Up and breakfast. Girls can get their own breakfast. They might have orange juice, French toast, cocoa. They can manage by themselves and usually do a good job both with breakfast and with cleaning up the kitchen, dining room, and sleeping quarters.

11:00 A.M. Taken home by hostess's mother.

Expenses

$12 to $15 should cover all expenses. This expenditure is almost entirely for food.

Hints and Warnings

Probably the most important thing is for the parents of the hostess to be temperamentally suited to stand all this giggling and foolishness and mess. They need to be able to stand it and to keep out of things.

It is also important, if possible, to have space so that all of this activity is not going on right in the middle of the family living.

If the girls go out for perhaps two hours in the early evening, this prevents the party from going stale before it gets started. It also prevents boys from finding out about the party and collecting to add to the confusion.

Be sure to have *plenty* of food. For instance, have both chocolate and white cake. Many cannot eat chocolate because of complexions—though others will gorge on it, while at the same time complaining about what it will do to their complexions.

Adults should try not to worry about the physical mess which is produced as the party proceeds. Most girls are quite capable of cleaning it all up nicely in the morning.

Adults should of course also not worry about the lack of sleep, or keep feeling that the girls should quiet down and sleep. Not sleeping and fooling around are practically the main point of the party.

However, you can try to avoid excessive mess by not having things around which will be too dangerous. (For instance, whipped cream containers, from which they might squirt whipped cream at each other, should be avoided, for this is the kind of humor which appeals to girls of this age.)

At this party, one of the main activities may be the planning of a future party, or of future parties. FOURTEENS love to plan parties, though some of the best parties may be those which spring up spontaneously, sometimes being thought of as late as 4 P.M. on the day the party is to be given. This has some advantages. It permits the party-givers to be a little more selective as to whom they invite, as the news of the party does not get out. It also can help to prevent party crashing.

FOURTEEN-YEAR-OLD BERMUDA SHORTS PARTY

A party like this may have sprung up more or less spontaneously, or may have been planned at a pajama party the preceding week. The hostess invites the girls who are her intimate friends, and each girl suggests the boy she would like to have invited.

All wear Bermuda shorts. This party may be just an after-dinner informal dancing party—dancing to records. It probably would last from 8 to 10 P.M.

Fourteen-Year-Old Bermuda Shorts Party

Refreshments could consist of homemade cookies, and punch made from lemonade and ginger ale.

Parents, as at other 14-year-old parties, are present but in the background. The party is very informal and the boys and girls run it. The parents, however, provide transportation.

After a party like this, girls may phone each other back and forth much of the next day to discuss what went on. The phoning and discussing may be the most important part of such a party.

FIFTEEN

The important thing about FIFTEEN and parties is not primarily, as at earlier ages, any special qualitative aspect of the personality at this age. True, FIFTEEN is often characterized as uncommunicative, withdrawn, blasé, argumentative, selfish, critical, rebellious. (More positively, as determined, discriminating, self-controlled.) But these characteristics, though presumably true of the individual at parties as at home, are not the main thing that a party-giver needs to keep in mind.

The thing we must remember in helping to plan a party for 15-year-olds is this. Earlier, say when a boy or girl is between the ages of two and ten years, even a relatively unpopular child can have a pretty good party because his parents can see to it that this is so. The success of the party depends, at these early ages, perhaps not so much on the personality of the child giving it as on careful and suitable planning by his parents.

Not so as the host or hostess approaches the teens. And by fifteen, especially, though there is still a good deal that parents can do to help, particularly in planning for and providing refreshments—the real success of the party seems to depend largely (even as at a grownup party) on the host and the guests themselves.

If the 15-year-old party-giver is popular and/or has a lively group of friends whom he can invite, his party, barring unforeseen calamities, is likely to be successful. If he doesn't have any friends, or if his friends (and thus his guests) are stuffy, self-conscious, shy, or poor mixers, in spite of any parental help or planning the party is likely to be stiff and not much fun.

The other main aspect of the age which has a bearing on parties and party-giving is the independence of the typical 15-year-old. FIFTEEN wants to plan and to run his own party. Parents can be useful as caterers, carriers, transporters, financial backers, and remote-control chaperons. But they no longer need or are permitted to play a leading role. It is most important for any adult helpers to conduct themselves inconspicuously and not try to take part in the party. Guests will speak and act politely to adults in charge, if and when they notice them—but that is all.

FIFTEEN-YEAR-OLD PARTY

Key

Even more so than at the age just preceding, the key to a successful party is to let the boy or girl giving the party make the plans. The adult role now is that of catering, providing, and chaperoning without getting in the way.

The success of the party now depends more on the host and guests. If they are a lively group who know each other well and have a good time together, the party is almost certain to go well. If they are a stiff group, or are mostly strangers to each other, there is not too much that adults can do to make the party a real success. Thus, though good planning and arranging are important, much more now probably depends on who is invited.

NUMBER OF GUESTS: At this age it is important to invite guests in couples. Six to eight couples is a good number.

NUMBER OF ADULTS: Since the main thing the adults need to do, besides somewhat remote chaperoning, is to provide food—and since the food is mostly prepared in advance—the party-giving parents could probably manage alone. One extra adult or one other adult couple, however, can be of considerable help right at the time the buffet supper is being served; and can also provide moral support for the parents.

Schedule

Good party hours are from 6:30 to 11. This works out especially well if the weather and the setting provide for outdoor, pre-supper games—or if there is a good recreation room for games. Otherwise, guests might come a little later, say at 7:00, and have supper fairly soon after their arrival. The party schedule can now be very simple, with time divided into big activity blocks.

6:30–7:30   Informal games. Such activities as ping-pong or archery are good. They provide an excellent outlet for energy, allow for participation or nonparticipation as any individual guest prefers, involve some element of competition and opportunity to exhibit special skills. They do not require rigid rules.

7:30–8:30 Refreshments, which still make up an extremely important part of any party. Refreshments need to be plentiful and filling, and may be served buffet style.

They may include hot dogs and hamburgers, rolls, milk and soft drinks, potato salad, tossed green salad. Also things to nibble on—available also before the formal eating starts—carrots, olives, celery, radishes.

The dessert can, if the guests like the idea, be a surprise dessert brought by the girls. This works out especially successfully if the girls know each other well enough to get together in planning and making this surprise.

8:30–11:00 Now comes the main feature of the evening—informal dancing to the record player. There is less confusion than at earlier ages about which records will be played. The group knows its own tastes, which are more or less shared by all. Differences of opinion are met with interest or ridicule, but do not cause serious difficulties.

There is also little of the earlier difficulty about getting the boys to dance. Many of the couples dance well and very much enjoy dancing with each other.

Also, by now most are relaxed enough about social affairs to be able to dance or not dance without stiffness or embarrassment. One couple, or several couples, may prefer to sit out a dance and just talk. Or a single guest if momentarily alone may merely pick up a book or magazine, without seeming too left out. Or two girls may momentarily get together and giggle.

Fruit punch and cookies are served very informally around 9:30 or 10 o'clock.

11:00 Departure. Since most of the boys do not as yet have their driving licenses, since many parents, and some states, restrict teen-age night driving, and since many do not really want to leave when it is time to go, it works out best if parents call for guests and drive them home.

Expenses

Expenses at this party are chiefly for food. Presumably the host will own (or can borrow) phonograph and records and any equipment

"Cueing up"

"Oops!"

Without a cue

Refreshments

Interludes

Contrasting moods

Going home

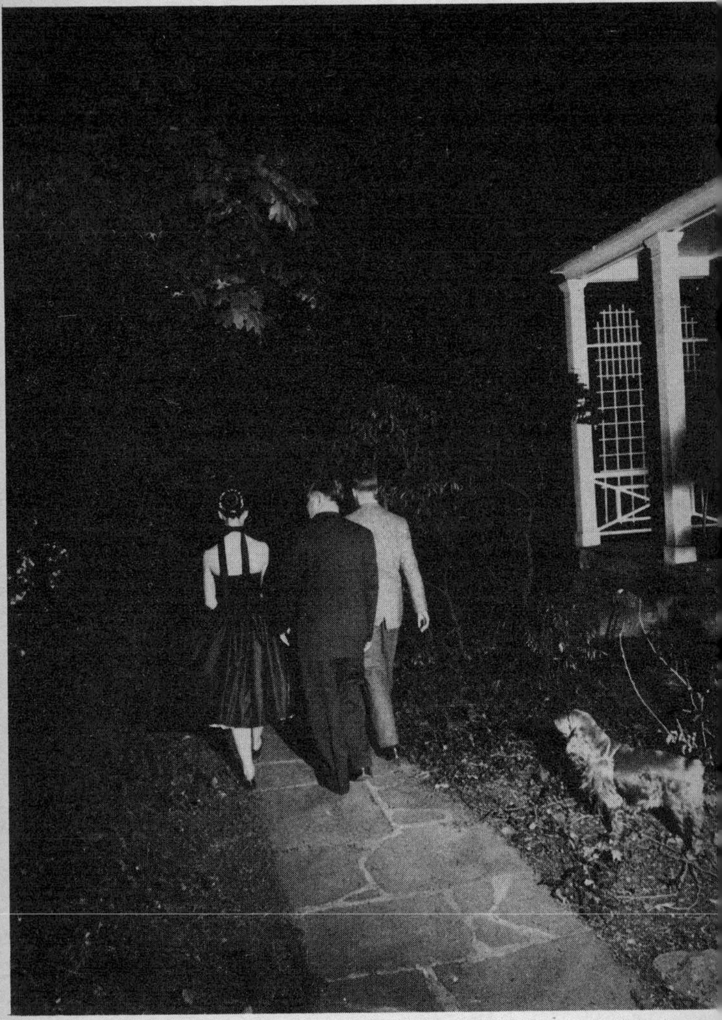

needed for archery and other games. Expense for food will vary with the type of menu, but will approximate what it would cost to feed a similar number of adult guests.

Hints and Warnings

It is essential to keep in mind that parents are not an important part of the party so far as the guests are concerned. In fact, adults are more or less invisible from the guests' point of view. However, parents are still essential at least during the early hours. Not only is there a good deal of providing and catering to do, if things are to go well, but most FIFTEENS are not old enough or responsible enough to see that things go smoothly.

The adults, of course, should not hover about or interfere. It is not necessarily something to worry about, for instance, if dancing occasionally dies down, so long as the guests seem reasonably well occupied. For the most part, FIFTEENS can manage by themselves and do not need to be helped, or encouraged, or organized. However, the adult must use his judgment and be able to differentiate between a normal and temporary lapse in activity, and a lapse which indicates that the party may have gone dead and may require desperate revival measures from the adults.

All of this requires some tact and skill on the part of the adults, who must be there when needed and out of the way when not needed. Toward the end of the evening, when and if it seems quite certain that the party is a success, adult chaperons can safely retire to some reasonably remote part of the house.

It is best at this age not to have the party too large. Much of its success will depend on the fact that guests know each other and are interested in each other. For this reason it is especially best not to invite too many outsiders. A school roommate (if some of the guests are "away" at school) or one or two out-of-town guests may liven things up; but too many outsiders are quite certain to spoil the flow of the party.

We have described here a planned and somewhat formal supper and dancing party. However, at fifteen (and increasingly at sixteen) years, many of the best parties come about without much planning. They may take place after a dance, or just after an evening "date," when couples who like each other get together at somebody's house. Such parties of course should not take place without reasonable chaperonage. In fact, parents and daughters (these parties are usually at the girls' houses) should have a general understanding about such parties and this understanding should include matters of chaperonage, refreshments, hours.

GENERAL SUGGESTIONS FOR ALL AGES

1. At any age, the more homogeneous the age grouping, the better things are likely to work out. This is true all the way along, at older as well as at younger ages. Also, younger siblings can be a real problem at any party. The ideal solution is to have them elsewhere. But if you must include them (that is, if they would be too hurt if excluded), realize that this will probably make the party more difficult, and plan accordingly. Special plans may be needed to work around siblings.

2. Note carefully party instructions under the individual ages to determine at which ages it is important for guests' mothers to be present at the party, and at which ages things tend to go best without the mothers. Similarly, note carefully at which age it is permissible, or even desirable, to have both girl and boy guests, and at which ages things tend to go best with either all girls or all boys.

   Since, even through fifteen, the help of at least one set of parents will be needed (but their role will be changing) one of the most important things is for parents to be aware in advance of what their role will be for each different age party, and what the children's response to them is likely to be.

3. At youngest ages it is especially important not to try to make parties too formal. Remember that the very young may be well satisfied with a party situation which to the adult may not seem to have too much shape to it.

   From seven to ten years, it is extremely important to keep children well occupied at all times, with situations which the adult plans and provides, so that they will become neither too wild nor, at the opposite extreme, too bored. As a rule it works out best to have active and quiet games alternate.

   In the teens, specific minute-to-minute planning becomes gradually less necessary. By fifteen, quite broad areas of activity can be planned and much flexibility permitted, and expected, depending on the guests' own spontaneous interests.

4. Remember that during the earliest years, a party situation is not the occasion for enforcing manners. Parties often bring out the worst in very young children, and therefore disputes and difficulties should be solved as simply as possible—often by separating contenders; and no attempt should be made to give lessons in manners. Some chil-

dren, often those who like the idea of parties most, nevertheless become overstimulated and tend to "go to pieces" at their own parties. In such cases, a birthday may be better celebrated merely by inviting some friend in to play, and serving birthday refreshments.

5. Through eight years of age, at any party where prizes and presents are given, it is important to provide a large paper or plastic bag with a name on it, so that each child can have something in which to keep all the things which belong to him. Then they will all be together and *safe*. . . . Have plenty of prizes and presents for all, particularly at the younger ages. However, keep the cost of individual favors and prizes down. Remember that each one has to be multiplied by the total number of guests.

Though some of the parties suggested here are moderately expensive, lack of money for favors, prizes, decorations, refreshments need not keep a party from being successful. All of these things can be kept simple and (except for food) at a minimum. Much more important than an expenditure of money in making a party a success is the homogeneity of guests and suitability of activities suggested for the maturity level of the children attending.

For many games, like Pin the Tail on the Donkey (or its seasonal variations) for instance, it is not essential to buy the equipment. It can be made at home without too much difficulty. Also, homemade party hats are often sturdier and last better than the store-bought varieties. Balloon pumps can be purchased inexpensively and are indispensable for blowing up balloons.

7. At any age, *anything* that needs to be prepared should be thoroughly prepared well in advance. It should not be necessary to go scrambling around at the last minute, or even after the guests have come, for things that are needed in games and activities.

8. Keep in mind in your planning, in the early years, that any or all guests may fail to turn up because of communicable diseases, broken limbs, weather, lack of transportation, or lack of baby sitters to free mothers for transporting. Or that the whole party—if an outdoor party—may have to be postponed because of weather.

9. It is most important to keep in mind not only the varying social maturity of individual children at any age, but also the social sophistication of the community in which you live. Thus, a party which would be suitable for 12- or 14-year-olds in one community might be too sophisticated for another. Your own child's interests, and those of his friends, can be your guide as to whether or not the party

suggested by us at any given age seems suitable, or whether you need something more advanced, or simpler.

We would especially suggest that parents of young adolescents first read over rules for all the different kinds of parties described in the 12- to 15-year age range, and then discuss arrangements with the boy or girl giving the party, before making definite plans. In these ages, particularly, suitable activities will vary greatly, especially depending upon the group's maturity so far as heterosexual relationships are concerned.

REFERENCES

1. HAMSHER, FLORENCE, *Party Cues for Teens*, Garden City Books, Garden City, New York, 1957.
*2. *Handbook for Recreation Leaders*, Publication 231, Federal Security Agency, Social Security Administration, Children's Bureau. Supt. of Documents, U.S. Govt. Printing Office, Washington, D.C.
3. HARBIN, E. O., *Games for Boys and Girls*, Abingdon Press, New York, 1951.
4. HARTLEY, RUTH E., and GOLDENSON, ROBERT M., *The Complete Book of Children's Play*, Thomas Y. Crowell Co., New York, 1957.
5. HOGAN, BERNICE, *Preschool Party Parade*, Abingdon, 1958.
6. KAPLER, HAZEL, *The Child and His Play*, Funk and Wagnalls Co., New York, 1952.
7. KOHL, MARGUERITE, and YOUNG, FREDERICA, *Parties for Children*, Hill and Wang, New York, 1958.
8. KRAUS, RICHARD, *Play Activities for Boys and Girls*, McGraw-Hill Book Co., Inc., New York, 1957.
*9. *Lawn Games for 4H Boys and Girls*, New York State College of Agriculture, Ithaca, New York.
10. LEEMING, JOSEPH, *The Real Book of Games*, Garden City Books, Garden City, New York, 1953.
11. McKENZIE, D., and RAYMOND, J. MOTYER, *Parties for Preschoolers*, Univ. of Toronto Press, Toronto, 1958.
*12. MILLEN, NINA, *Children's Games from Many Lands*, Friendship Press, New York, 1943.
13. MULAC, MARGARET, and HOLMES, MARIAN, *The Party Game Book*, Harper & Brothers, New York, 1951.
*14. *Program of Songs, Games, and Folk Dances for 4–14 Clubs*, New York State College of Agriculture, Ithaca, New York.
15. SMITH, LAURA ROUNDTREE, *200 Games that Teach*, Beckley-Cordy Co., Chicago, 1923.
16. YOUNG, WILLIAM P., and GARDINER, HORACE J., *Games and Stunts for all Occasions*, J. P. Lippincott, New York, 1935. (12 years and up)

* These were taken from the exhaustive bibliography in Reference 4.

The Gesell Institute's
CHILD BEHAVIOR

By FRANCES L. ILG, M.D.

and LOUISE BATES AMES, PH.D.

*A realistic guide to child behavior
in vital formative years from birth to ten*

Here at last is a book—the first from the famous Gesell Institute of Child Development to give specific what-to-do advice—that is both relaxed and authoritative, designed to help and to reassure parents in their unending search for the right answers.

"The Gesell Institute is America's foremost authority on child development." —A.M.A. Journal

"A mass of wonderful, helpful, useful information." —Chicago Tribune

"A milestone in education. Gesell is to older children what Spock is to babies. Buy it." —P.T.A. Magazine

A DELL LAUREL EDITION 60¢